"Nancy Guthrie is one of the best teachers of Scripture I've ever heard or read. Her style—even in writing—is conversational. It's like you're sharing a cup of coffee while tracing the central motifs of the biblical story from Genesis to Revelation. Eden was great, but the new creation will be greater than the first—not because this world will be no more, but because it will be so much more. It's not only the end of sin and death, but the kind of righteousness and life that we just can't wrap our brain around right now. But we do get glimpses—and no better ones than those that Guthrie brings out with such warmth, excitement, and skill."

Michael Horton, J. Gresham Machen Professor of Theology and Apologetics, Westminster Seminary California; Cohost, *White Horse Inn*; author, *Core Christianity*

"*Even Better than Eden* weaves a glorious tapestry of variegated scriptural threads. Nancy Guthrie traces nine magnificent threads from creation to consummation that provide an accessible primer on the biblical metanarrative. Each thread, when unraveled, reveals the beauty and splendor of Jesus. The pages of this book fill me with an eager anticipation of the day when we will get to our home that will be even better than Eden and the completed work of art will be unveiled in all its glory."

Karen Hodge, Women's Ministry Coordinator, Presbyterian Church in America

"One of the weaknesses of much popular Christian teaching on the Bible is the tendency to read the story of the Bible in a circular manner, as if Jesus Christ came into the world to bring us back to Eden. Nancy Guthrie charts a better course in her book. In a manner that is profoundly biblical and deeply practical, she traces nine biblical themes along a common trajectory, from their beginning in God's good creation, through their destruction and devastation by Adam's sin, to the ways Christ perfects, consummates, and crowns each theme by means of his suffering and glory. Let Guthrie take you by the hand and lead you through the Bible to Jesus Christ, in whom we find a better provision, a better life, a better identity, a better rest, a better wardrobe, a better spouse, a better savior, a better sanctuary, and a better city than this world in its present state could or would afford."

Scott Swain, President and James Woodrow Hassell Professor of Systematic Theology, Reformed Theological Seminary, Orlando

"As a pastor, I have discovered that Christians need help learning to tell their own story in ways that rightly connect it to what God has preserved for us in his Word. With *Even Better than Eden*, Nancy Guthrie does just that. Here is a book that will train you to speak more winsomely to others about why and how Jesus matters."

David Helm, Pastor, Holy Trinity Church, Chicago; author, *The Big Picture Story Bible*

"This delightful book will help you see—through new eyes—the beautiful threads in the rich tapestry of the Bible's story. I will be recommending this insightful and informative book to many."

Jonathan Gibson, Assistant Professor of Old Testament, Westminster Theological Seminary, Philadelphia, Pennsylvania

Even Better than Eden

Even Better than Eden

Nine Ways the Bible's Story Changes Everything about Your Story

Nancy Guthrie

:: CROSSWAY®

WHEATON, ILLINOIS

Library of Congress Cataloging-in-Publication Data
Names: Guthrie, Nancy, author.
Title: Even better than Eden : nine ways the Bible's story changes everything / Nancy Guthrie.
Description: Wheaton : Crossway, 2018. | Includes bibliographical references and index.
Identifiers: LCCN 2018000252 (print) | LCCN 2018026076 (ebook) | ISBN 9781433561269 (pdf) | ISBN 9781433561276 (mobi) | ISBN 9781433561283 (epub) | ISBN 9781433561252 (tp)
Subjects: LCSH: Kingdom of God. | Jesus Christ—Kingdom. | Eschatology. | Heaven—Christianity. | Bible—Theology.
Classification: LCC BT94 (ebook) | LCC BT94 .G875 2018 (print) | DDC 231.7—dc23
LC record available at https://lccn.loc.gov/2018000252

Crossway is a publishing ministry of Good News Publishers.

LB   29   28   27   26   25   24   23   22   21   20   19
15   14   13   12   11   10   9   8   7   6   5   4   3

As a woman who has so much to learn and yet seeks to faithfully teach the Bible, I have been so blessed to be surrounded by the sound teaching, personal encouragement, helpful input, and gentle critique of a number of theologically trained men, and I am so very grateful.

Thank you, Dr. James Walters, for lighting a fire in me at John Brown University with the first paper you assigned in Christian Life class on the glory of God.

Thank you, Ray Ortlund Jr., for introducing me to biblical theology and to what it means to be graciously Reformed.

Thank you, Jean Larroux, for being the first to listen through one of my messages and affirm its clear presentation of the gospel.

Thank you, David Filson, for being so brilliant that I just had to talk through with you the ideas for this book before I got started, for encouraging me at every step along the way, and for commending me to others beyond my true capability.

Thank you, Matt Bradley (and Leslie!), for your careful reading of this manuscript and for the kind of careful feedback I've always wanted before sending a book out into the world.

Thank you, Nate Shurden, for being such a wise and faithful shepherd to your flock, for faithfully praying for me and my ministry, and for being a constant resource and encouragement.

Finally, thank you to those theologians who helped me so much with this project through recorded lectures, sermons, articles, and books. I'm especially grateful to Greg Beale, J. V. Fesko, Ligon Duncan, Michael Horton, and Lane Tipton.

Personal Bible study questions for each chapter and a leader's guide that includes possible answers to the personal Bible study and discussion guide questions are available for download at http://www.nancyguthrie.com/even-better-than-eden.

Contents

Introduction

If I were to tell you my story, I'd probably tell you about where my life began: in Kansas City, Missouri; about my parents: Claude and Ella Dee; and about my husband, David, and children, Matt, Hope, and Gabriel. I might tell you about significant events in my life: where I grew up, where I went to college and began my career, how I met and married David, how my life changed when my son Matt was born, and then changed even more when my children Hope and Gabriel died. I'd tell you where I live—in Nashville—and what I do there day to day: write and teach, avoid the grocery store and the gym, walk in the park with my friends, do the laundry, answer emails, edit my podcast, go to church, make dinner, watch more TV than I'd care to admit, and go to bed. All those things would tell you true things about me and my story. But they simply wouldn't be the most significant aspects of my story. They simply wouldn't be the most profound realities that have shaped my past, my present, or my future.

There's another story, a story that is found in the pages of the Bible—from the book of Genesis through the book of Revelation—that shapes and defines where I came from, why I am the way I am, what my life is like day to day, and what is ahead for me in the future. It is this story that explains my deepest joys as well as the empty places where contentment can be elusive. It is this story that explains my drive to be somebody and my sensitivity to feeling like a nobody. It explains what makes me cry and why I can laugh. This story explains my desire to look good, my craving for the good life, my longing for home and security, and much more.

And whether you know it or not, this same grand story—the story found in the sixty-six books of the Bible—shapes the world you live in, who you are, and what you want too. That's why you and I need to know this story. It is where we find the answers to our questions about what really matters now and into eternity. This story has the power to change everything about our stories.

Eden: Where Your Story Begins

The story of the Bible begins in Genesis 1 with God creating the heavens and the earth and putting Adam and Eve in a garden called Eden. Eden was bright and beautiful, and we tend to think of it in perfect and even ultimate terms. We often talk about our desires for the future as the restoration of Eden or returning to Eden. But the reality is, the Eden we read about in Genesis 1 and 2 wasn't yet everything God intended for his creation. It was unsullied but incomplete. It was bursting with potential, but it wasn't yet all that God intended for the home he would share with his people. From the very beginning Eden was not meant to be static; it was headed somewhere.[1] Likewise, Adam and Eve were not yet all that God intended for his people to be. They were sinless but not yet glorious, at least not as glorious as God intended them to become. Something better was held out to Adam and Eve if they obeyed God's Word to them.

But the sad story of Eden is that Adam and Eve did not obey. Everything in Eden went terribly wrong. This is the part of the Bible's story that explains why so much goes so terribly wrong in our stories. This is the part of the story that provides the most profound answer to our *why* questions in the hurts and hardships in our lives.

Fortunately, however, the story that began in Eden did not end there. God's plan for his world and his people could not be thwarted by human sin. God is, even now, working out his plan to do far more than simply restore his creation to the state of integrity that was Eden. Christ came to accomplish what was necessary to open the way for us, not just back into the garden of Eden, but into a home that will be even better than Eden and a life that will be even better than the life Adam and Eve enjoyed there.

How will it be better? That's what this book is all about. Every chapter will trace a theme that runs from Genesis to Revelation and that reveals an aspect of the excellencies and superiorities of the new heaven and the new earth (which we could also call Eden 2.0, or the new Eden, or the new creation, or the city to come, or the New Jerusalem)—superior not only to life in this sin-affected world we live in now, but superior even to what Adam and Eve experienced in the original Eden.

But this book is not focused solely on what is to come when Christ returns and establishes the new heaven and the new earth, because the glory, the life, the intimacy, the security, and the newness of that future is not solely reserved for the future. We aren't yet experiencing it in the full and complete way we one day will, but it is breaking into the here and now. Think of the way Mark begins his Gospel by telling us the good news that Jesus began to tell at the start of his ministry. Jesus said, "The kingdom of God is at hand." With Christ's incarnation, the newness that comes only from him began breaking into this world. Then, in his resurrection, this newness began flooding into the world. And it is still flooding into the world as the gospel goes out and is embraced by people from every nation. The power of the gospel still brings life where there is death, hope where there is despair, beauty where there is brokenness.

As the gospel goes out and people take hold of the risen Christ by faith, the new creation continues to transform this world. This is what Paul was talking about when he wrote: "If anyone is in Christ, the new creation has come: The old has gone, the new is here!" (2 Cor. 5:17 NIV). In other words, to be joined to the risen Christ is to have the newness and glory and life of the greater Eden breaking into your life in the here and now. Taking hold of the glory of the future transforms your sense of shame now. A settled sense of the security of the future soothes your fear of death now. A growing sense of identity as a citizen of heaven changes how you see yourself now. Truly taking in the love relationship we're going to enjoy forever warms our hearts toward Christ now.

Paul wrote that we are those "on whom the end of the ages has come" (1 Cor. 10:11). And if that is true, we want to understand more about the end of the ages. We want to see what the original garden has to show us about the more secure, more satisfying, and more glorious garden we're destined to live in forever, which will be even better than Eden.

1

The Story of the Wilderness

I promise you: I am the last person in the world who should attempt to teach you a word in another language. I took two years of German in high school and two semesters of it in college, and all I can remember is *ich bin*, which means, "I am." I can't even remember enough German to make a complete sentence out of those words. Once after I spoke in a women's prison in Colombia, South America, I wanted to be able to greet each woman as she picked up the small gift we had for her and to say, "The Lord loves you," in Spanish. But I just couldn't keep it straight. My husband, David, had to stand behind me and repeat the Spanish phrase over and over because I kept getting off track. Who knows what I said to those women?

But there is a Hebrew phrase I want to teach you because it adds such dimension to the story the Bible tells, beginning with the first sentence in the Bible. And besides, it's kind of fun to say. Ready? Here it is: *tohu wabohu* (תהו ובהו).

It's there, in the opening sentences of the Bible. Our English Bible reads, "In the beginning, God created the heavens and the earth. The earth was without form and void, and darkness was over the face of the deep" (Gen. 1:1–2). The Bible begins by saying that God created the heavens and the earth and that it was, in Hebrew, *tohu wabohu*. It was "without form and void" or "formless and empty" (NIV). *Tohu* means "unformed, chaotic wilderness," and *bohu* means "empty." So Genesis 1:2 tells us that when God created the heavens and the earth, it was initially an uninhabitable wasteland, a barren wilderness. There was no shape or form to it. No life could live in it.

I suppose I've always thought that when God created the earth, he spoke it into existence as it is. But evidently what God spoke into being was initially a mass of unformed matter in which nothing and no one could live. It was the raw materials to which God would give shape and form. In fact, there were three significant problems with the earth as God initially created it, according to Genesis 1:2. It was formless, empty, and dark. But it was not without hope. Why? Because "the Spirit of God was hovering over the face of the waters" (Gen 1:2).

The Spirit of God was there hovering—or fluttering—over the deep darkness of the unformed earth like a hen hovering over an unhatched cosmos.[1] Something was about to happen. God, by his Spirit, through his Word, was about to illumine and order and fill his creation.

So right there in the first chapter of the Bible we discover that *tohu wabohu* is not a problem for God. As his word, "Let there be," goes out, and as the Spirit's creative energy hovers, what was dark was flooded with light, what was chaotic came to order, and what was empty was filled with life and beauty and purpose.

This is really good news. Because, although you may have been unfamiliar with the term *tohu wabohu*, the reality of it may be achingly familiar. Perhaps you sense that the deepest, most honest place inside you is *tohu wabohu*—a dark and brooding emptiness. Perhaps it is an emptiness brought about by loss. There was once something or someone that filled up that space in your life, but now your heart aches with longing for what once was. Now there is an empty place at the table or an empty room in the house, or you sleep in an empty bed. Instead of having plans and a sense of purpose, an empty schedule and future loom before you. Or perhaps the emptiness in your life is punctuated not by what once was but by what has never been. There has never been a ring on your finger or a child in your womb or a title by your name. The dreams you have often sought to downplay for fear that saying them out loud would somehow serve to crush them, and thereby crush you, seem to be out of range or the realm of possibility. Or perhaps you can't pinpoint exactly why you have this sense of emptiness. You realize that in comparison to so many others around you, you have it good. Yet your soul harbors a nagging sense of disappointment and discontentment. It sometimes seems as if the lives of nearly everyone around you are full of purpose and meaning, life and love, fun times and future plans, which serve to punctuate the empty place in your life.

Sometimes your sense of emptiness haunts you as a nagging ache. At other times it overwhelms you as a relentless agony. Perhaps you have come to see your emptiness as your biggest problem. I have to tell you: that's not how God sees it. God sees the emptiness in your life as his greatest opportunity, because God does his best work with *empty* as he fills it with himself.

Discontentment in the Garden

Adam and Eve had no reason to feel a sense of emptiness. Their world was filled with so much goodness. Everywhere they looked, they encountered what God had spoken into being and declared to be good and even very good. He put them in a garden paradise where he had planted every kind of tree that was good for food. God simply spoke, "Let the earth sprout vegetation, plants yielding seed, and fruit trees bearing fruit in which is their seed, each according to its kind, on the earth" (Gen. 1:11). And it was so. And God saw that it was good.

Anyone who has struggled to get a tree or shrub to take root in resistant ground or spent a day pulling weeds in the garden, only to see them choking out your sweet strawberries, or anyone who has tried to chase the moles to the next-door neighbor's yard (who would do such a thing?) can hardly imagine what this must have been like. Nothing turned brown and wilted away or dried up in Eden. The prick of a thorn never sent Adam looking for a Band-Aid. Adam and Eve were given the work of filling the earth, subduing it, and exercising dominion over it. In the same way that God brought order to the initial chaos of his creation, Adam was to extend the order of Eden. Together, Adam and Eve were to be fruitful and multiply so that their progeny would extend the boundaries of Eden, filling it with men and women who, like Adam and Eve, bore the image of their Creator so that "the earth will be filled with the knowledge of the glory of the LORD as the waters cover the sea" (Hab. 2:14).

There was no lack in Adam and Eve's lives; they had every reason to be perfectly content. Yet when the Serpent suggested to Eve that there was something she didn't have, something she really needed to be happy, namely, the wisdom that would come from eating from the forbidden tree and the taste experience of eating its delicious fruit, Eve allowed the perspective of the Serpent to shape her perspective. Rather than being content with all the goodness showered on her and surrounding her, Eve began to see an empty place in her life, in her diet, in her knowledge, in her experience. Her desire for something more, something other than God's provision, combined with her growing doubts about God's goodness, led her to reach out for what she thought would make her happy, fulfilled, and satisfied.

Oh, how that bite must have turned sour in her stomach as the reality of what she had done worked its way through her. Oh, how that grab for wisdom must have seemed so foolish on the other side of it. When God turned from cursing the Serpent toward telling Eve and Adam how this curse was going to affect them, it must have become clear that what she had seen as a delight was actually a disaster. The very things that were supposed to bring them so much joy and satisfaction would now bring pain and frustration. Giving birth to children and raising children in the now sin-infected world would be painful. Her one-flesh marriage to Adam would now be filled with friction. Adam's work would be frustrating instead of fulfilling. Adam was meant to till the soil. But now it would become painful toil. The ground would grow fruit, but it would also grow thorns, thorns that would penetrate Adam's flesh.

That flicker of discontentment that Eve had entertained in the garden must have become a raging fire after she and Adam were exiled into the unsubdued wilderness that surrounded it.[2] But the chronic discontentment that now dogged her also proved to be a grace. It proved to be a constant reminder that complete and lasting contentment exists only in the life that was promised to them had they obeyed, had they been able to feast forever on the fruit of the tree of life. But how would they get it now? Angels were there on watch, guarding the way back into the garden.

God himself would make a way for his people to enter into a garden even better than Eden. He began by calling to himself one man living in Ur—Abraham—to live in the land God would give him. There was no angel guarding the entrance to that land when Abraham entered it, but, interestingly, when his grandson Jacob later left that land to get a wife, he wrestled with an angel on his way back in. By the end of Jacob's life, his sons were not living in the land but were enslaved in Egypt. So God sent a deliverer who announced to God's people that he had "come down to deliver them out of the hand of the Egyptians and to bring them up out of that land to a good and broad land, a land flowing with milk and honey" (Ex. 3:8). Kind of sounds like a new Eden, doesn't it?

Discontentment in the Wilderness

Unfortunately, the pathway to this edenic land took a forty-year detour in the wilderness. It was there that the discontentment inherent to life in the wilderness raised its ugly head. We read about it in the book we call Numbers but which was originally titled, "In the Wilderness." Moses tells us:

> Now the rabble that was among them had a strong craving. And the people of Israel also wept again and said, "Oh that we had meat to eat! We remember the fish we ate in Egypt that cost

nothing, the cucumbers, the melons, the leeks, the onions, and the garlic. But now our strength is dried up, and there is nothing at all but this manna to look at." (Num. 11:4–6)

It's not that they had nothing to eat. It's that they wanted something else to eat besides the manna God rained down on them every day. Their stomachs, in reality, were not empty. But they felt a sense of emptiness nonetheless. And it sounds a little familiar, doesn't it? Like Adam and Eve, who were free to eat of every tree in the garden except for one—yet they felt deprived? (And like me when I order Diet Coke, and the waiter says, "Will Diet Pepsi be all right?")

Forty years after the Israelites first allowed their appetites to give way to grumbling, as their children prepared to emerge from the wilderness into the land God had promised to give to them, Moses explained why God had let them experience empty stomachs in the first place: "He humbled you and let you hunger and fed you with manna, which you did not know, nor did your fathers know, *that he might make you know* that man does not live by bread alone, but man lives by every word that comes from the mouth of the LORD" (Deut. 8:3).

He "let you hunger." He allowed them to feel their emptiness. Why? So that their hunger pangs, their discontentment, would cause them to consider carefully what would deeply satisfy them, what would fill them up. It wasn't merely spicy food. It was a divine word, a divine presence, a divine promise, a divine power for living with less than everything they might want in the wilderness of this world.

Have you ever thought about the emptiness you feel in this light? Do you think, perhaps, that God has let you hunger for whatever it is you are so hungry for so that you might become more desperate for him, more convinced that he is the source of what will fill you up? Do you think he might want to retrain your appetites, redirecting them away from this world, this life, even this age, so that your anticipation of the age to come might begin to shape your perspective on whatever it is you lack?

As they prepared to enter the land, Moses passed along this promise from God to his people:

> If you will indeed obey my commandments that I command you today, to love the LORD your God, and to serve him with all your heart and with all your soul, he will give the rain for your land in its season, the early rain and the later rain, that you may gather in your grain and your wine and your oil. And he will give grass in your fields for your livestock, and you shall eat and be full. Take care lest your heart be deceived, and you turn aside and serve other gods and worship them; then the anger of the LORD will be kindled against you, and he will shut up the heavens, so that there will be no rain, and the land will yield no fruit, and you will perish quickly off the good land that the LORD is giving you. (Deut. 11:13–17)

Oh, how we wish that they had learned the lessons they were meant to learn during those forty years in the wilderness. Evidently they didn't. Rather than living by every word that comes from the mouth of the Lord, they consumed everything served up to them by the Canaanites living in the land. What Moses had warned them would happen if they refused to obey God became their harsh reality. God used the Babylonian army to bring judgment on his people. In the wake of their destruction, the land of milk and honey became a wilderness. The prophet Jeremiah described what Israel was like after the armies of Babylon descended on it:

> I looked on the earth, and behold, it was *without form and void*;
>   and to the heavens, and they had no light. . . .
> I looked, and behold, the fruitful land was a desert,
>   and all its cities were laid in ruins
>   before the LORD, before his fierce anger. (Jer. 4:23, 26)

Did you see our new Hebrew phrase, *tohu wabohu*, in there? Jeremiah borrows language from Genesis 1:2 to describe the condition of Judah under the devastating destruction of the Babylonian army. The land had once again become "without form and void"—*tohu wabohu*. They'd been given a land of milk and honey, and it had become a barren wasteland. Empty of beauty. Empty of life. Empty of joy.

But this was not the end of the story. Jeremiah was also given a vision of what was to come when God's people would leave behind their wilderness existence in Babylon to come home. Jeremiah prophesied, "They shall come and sing aloud on the height of Zion, and they shall be radiant over the goodness of the LORD, over the grain, the wine, and the oil, and over the young of the flock and the herd; their life shall be *like a watered garden,* and they shall languish no more" (Jer. 31:12).

A "watered garden"? How would this happen? When would this happen?

Contentment in the Wilderness

Real restoration began centuries later with the sound of a single voice, the voice of the messenger, John the Baptist:

> The voice of one crying in the wilderness:
> "Prepare the way of the Lord;
>   make his paths straight." (Matt. 3:3)

Just as the Spirit hovered and the Word went out and the dark emptiness was filled with light and life at creation, so, at the dawn of the new creation, the same Spirit hovered over the dark emptiness of a virgin's womb. Mary was told: "The Holy Spirit will come upon you, and the power of the Most High will overshadow you; therefore the child to be born will be called holy—the Son of God" (Luke 1:35). Once again the Word went out, but this time instead of going out in creative power, it went out in human form. "And the Word became flesh and dwelt among us" (John 1:14). God flooded the world with his goodness by entering into it in the person of Jesus Christ.

Jesus, the second Adam, the true Israel, left the heavenly land of milk and honey and entered into the wilderness of this world with all of its thorns and thistles. We're meant to see it at the very beginning of his ministry: "Then Jesus was led up by the Spirit into the wilderness to be tempted by the devil" (Matt. 4:1). Just as Satan had entered the garden to tempt Adam and Eve, so the Devil entered into the wilderness to tempt Jesus. Just as Satan had twisted God's word, stoking the fires of discontentment with God's provision of food and suggesting that Adam and Eve could reach out and grab for themselves the glory God had promised rather than trusting God to give it to them, so Satan twisted God's word toward his own evil ends, suggesting that Jesus use his power to feed himself rather than trust in God's provision of food. He tempted Jesus to grab hold of glory by indulging himself rather than waiting for the glory that would come by submitting to the cross. But instead of falling prey to what the Tempter said, Jesus responded by quoting the words God had spoken through Moses to his people in the wilderness: "Man shall not live by bread alone, but by every word that comes from the mouth of God" (Matt. 4:4; cf. Deut. 8:3).

Matthew tells us that after Jesus passed the test of temptation in the wilderness, "angels came and were ministering to him" (Matt. 4:11). Such a different experience than that of the first Adam. The angels had stood against the first Adam as adversaries, preventing his return from the wilderness to the garden. And such a different result than the first Adam brought about. Because of the first Adam's failure to obey in a garden, all of humanity was plunged into the wilderness. But because of the second Adam's willingness to obey in the wilderness, the way back into a garden even better than Eden has been opened to us.

Jesus began assuring those who put their faith in him of this reality even as he hung on the cross, saying to the thief hanging beside him, "Truly, I say to you, today you will be with me in paradise" (Luke 23:43). There, on the cross, Jesus entered into the ultimate wasteland of death—the ultimate *tohu wabohu*—in our place, so that we might enter into the abundant life that God has promised.

We get a sense of new-garden life breaking into the wilderness of the world immediately upon the resurrection of Jesus. John tells us, "Now in the place where he was crucified there was a garden, and in the garden a new tomb in which no one had yet been laid" (John 19:41). He continues, "Mary stood weeping outside the tomb, and as she wept she stooped to look into the tomb. And she saw two angels in white, sitting where the body of Jesus had lain, one at the head and one at the feet" (John 20:11–12). It seems that this empty tomb had become the entryway into the new garden. Two angels were there to welcome in those who were willing to identify with Jesus in his death and resurrection. We read that Mary "turned around and saw Jesus standing, but she did not know that it was Jesus. Jesus said to her, 'Woman, why are you weeping? Whom are you seeking?' Supposing him to be the gardener . . ." (John 20:14–15).

"Supposing him to be the gardener . . ." And of course, he was—he is—the Gardener! This was the dawn of the new creation. The Gardener was up at the crack of this dawn doing the work the first Adam failed to do—extending the boundaries of paradise into the wilderness of this world.[3] Even now the new creation is breaking into the wilderness of our lives in this world. It happens when we identify with Jesus, when we become joined to Jesus in his death and resurrection. This is what Paul means when he says, "If anyone is in Christ, the new creation has come" (2 Cor. 5:17 NIV). It breaks into our lives and changes us from spiritually dead people into spiritually alive people, people who begin experiencing—in part now and in fullness forever—the unending, abundant, all-satisfying life that Adam and Eve would have enjoyed had they passed the probationary test of the tree in Eden.[4]

But even as I say that, perhaps you're thinking, "Yes, that sounds good, but my life is still marked in many ways by wilderness, disappointment, discontentment, emptiness." I get that. Mine is too. This reality makes us wonder if it is really possible to live in the wilderness of this world with any real sense of the new creation breaking in to our here and now. The apostle Paul's experience of both the thorns of the wilderness and the contentment of the garden to come would suggest it is.

Paul's way of expressing the pain in his life was, "I was given a thorn in my flesh" (2 Cor. 12:7 NIV). What was this thorn? We don't know. What we do know is that it was far more than a slight discomfort. The Greek word he used for *thorn* refers to a stake—a sharpened wooden shaft used to impale someone. So whatever this thorn was, Paul felt impaled, pinned down, by it. He recounts his repeated pleading with God to take it away. Clearly, whatever it was, it brought unrelenting agony.

Most of us, when we suffer, ask why. But Paul didn't ask why. He seemed to know exactly why the thorn in the flesh had been given to him and from where or—more precisely—from whom it came. Paul had been given a guided tour of paradise, the place where God dwells. Getting an advance glimpse of paradise is the kind of experience that could cause a person's head to swell with spiritual pride. "So to keep me from becoming conceited because of the surpassing greatness of the revelations, a thorn was given me in the flesh" (2 Cor. 12:7). When Paul looked at the thorn, he saw the hand of God at work in his life, protecting him from using his incredible spiritual experience to make himself look good. But clearly that's not all Paul saw in the thorn.

He also described the thorn in his flesh as "a messenger of Satan, to torment me" (NIV). Satan tormented Paul with the temptation to resent God for allowing the thorn to pierce his already pain-ridden life. He tormented Paul with the temptation to blame God and grow resentful. But it was clear to Paul that Satan was not ultimately in charge of the thorn. God, in his sovereign power, was at work using what Satan meant for evil for his own good purpose. Paul understood that God intended to use the thorn for a sanctifying purpose in his life.

But he still begged for the thorn to be removed, for the pain to stop. And I appreciate that. Even when we can see that God is using the hurts in our lives to accomplish something good in us, we still want the pain to stop. Paul begged God to take it away. And then he begged again. And then he begged again. And then he heard Jesus himself speak to him: "My grace is sufficient for you, for my power is made perfect in weakness" (2 Cor. 12:9).

Jesus's answer to Paul's righteous, rigorous, repeated prayer was not to take the thorn away but rather to provide Paul with enough grace to enable him to endure living with the thorn. Paul would experience divine power, not in the thorn being removed, but in its being redeemed. "Therefore I will boast all the more gladly of my weaknesses, so that the power of Christ may rest upon me," Paul wrote

(2 Cor. 12:9). Evidently this promise of "the power of Christ"—the same power that enabled Jesus to endure the cross, the same power that raised Jesus from the dead—coming to rest on him changed Paul's perspective about the thorn that was to continue to be a reality in his life day by day. This new perspective enabled him to say, "For the sake of Christ, then, I am *content* with weaknesses, insults, hardships, persecutions, and calamities. For when I am weak, then I am strong" (2 Cor. 12:10). Contentment in the wilderness. Contentment for now in a land where thorns produce pain.

Does this sound possible to you? Does it seem possible that you could be content even if your circumstances don't change? Does it seem possible that you could open up to receiving divine power that would change how you think about the empty places in your life?

My friend, if you are weak—worn out from work, worn down by criticism, weary of constant demands or disappointments—if you have come to the end of yourself, if you've been emptied of your delusions of strength, you're at just the right place to be filled with the goodness of God. You're finally fillable. You're fully dependent. There is room for the power of Christ to rest on you in such a way that it will give you the strength to be content even as you continue to live your life in the wilderness of this world.

"When I am weak, then I am strong." This was the reality that shaped Paul's life. But really Paul's life was just being conformed to the pattern of Christ's life. Jesus, the craftsman who made the world, entered into the wilderness of his world in weakness as an embryo in his mother's womb. "He was despised and rejected by men; / a man of sorrows and acquainted with grief" (Isa. 53:3). Jesus was insulted. "Can anything good come out of Nazareth?" (John 1:46). Jesus experienced hardships. "Foxes have holes, and birds of the air have nests, but the Son of Man has nowhere to lay his head" (Luke 9:58). Jesus faced persecution. "Then they spit in his face and struck him. And some slapped him" (Matt. 26:67). Jesus experienced calamities. "[Herod] sent and had John beheaded in the prison. . . . Now when Jesus heard this, he withdrew from there in a boat to a desolate place by himself" (Matt. 14:10, 13).

You see, Jesus not only entered into the wilderness the wilderness of this world entered into him. Jesus had a flesh—many thorns pressed into his tender flesh. And if) rienced a thorn in the flesh, and we've said that it is our desii lives to be conformed to his, joined to his, why are we so sui ..sed and even resentful when we feel the pain of a thorn in our flesh, when we experience the agonies of life lived in a world of wilderness?

People are so hungry for supernatural experiences—miracles of healing, visions and dreams, a personal word from God. Here is the supernatural experience that God has promised: the power of Christ coming down to rest on you, to fill you up, so that you can trust him when the worst thing you can imagine happens to you, so that you can be genuinely, if not yet perfectly, content even if he does not fill up the empty place in the way that you have longed for. At least not yet.

Contentment in the New Garden

You see, this is where the story of the Bible changes everything about your story, including the emptiness and discontentment in your story. The day is coming when thorns and thistles that are a tangible sign of the impact of the curse on this world, an ever-present part of living in the wilderness of this world, will be a thing of the past. Paul writes in Romans:

> For the creation waits with eager longing for the revealing of the sons of God. For the creation was subjected to futility, not willingly, but because of him who subjected it, in hope that the creation itself will be set free from its bondage to corruption and obtain the freedom of the glory of the children of God. (Rom. 8:19–21)

The apostle John was allowed to see a vision of what the world will be like when creation is set free from its bondage to corruption, when it experiences the same resurrection and renewal our bodies will experience when Christ returns and raises us from our graves with bodies fit for living in the new earth. In the very last chapter of the Bible, which describes the first chapter of life in the new garden that we'll be welcomed into, John tells us, "No longer will there be anything accursed" (Rev. 22:3). No more curse. No more thorns that bring pain. No more *tohu wabohu*. The goodness and glory of a garden even better than Eden will extend to every corner of the earth. And the goodness of God will fill up every part of you. No more disappointment. No more discontentment. All the empty places will be filled up, all your deepest longings fulfilled.

Until then we can sing:

Guide me, O thou great Jehovah,
Pilgrim through this barren land.
I am weak, but thou art mighty;
Hold me with thy powerful hand.
Bread of heaven, bread of heaven,
Feed me till I want no more.
Feed me till I want no more.[5]

2

The Story of the Tree

One of my favorite lines in a movie is delivered by Albert Brooks to William Hurt in *Broadcast News*. Hurt's character is a pretty-boy news anchor who has just been given a network job. He's talking to Brooks's character, who is brilliant and works hard but can't seem to get ahead. Hurt's character asks the question, "What do you do when your real life exceeds your dreams?" And Brooks's character replies in covetous disgust, "You keep it to yourself!"[1]

Anyone who has looked at pictures of someone else's seemingly perfect family or idyllic vacation on social media and felt a little jealous has been tempted to say the same thing. Most of us know what it is like to sense, at one time or another, that people around us seem to be living the good life while we can't seem to get there. We're not always sure what the good life is; we just sense the life we're living isn't it. The good life can seem like a mirage set out before us that is always just out of reach.

So what is the good life, and how do we get it?

Five of my favorite people in the world are Eric, Ruth, Abby, Brennan, and Pearl Brown. When Ruth was twenty weeks pregnant with Pearl, Pearl was diagnosed with alobar holoprosencephaly (HPE), a neural disease with low chances of survival. The doctor encouraged Eric and Ruth to induce labor and end the pregnancy. But the Browns opted to embrace life and hope and to carry Pearl to term. They didn't know how long she would live or what her life would be like, but it is now almost five years later, and Pearl is still very much alive! Their lives and Pearl's life aren't easy, but Pearl is so loved. The constant hospitalizations that have marked Pearl's life, Abby's recent diagnosis of juvenile diabetes, and foundation problems with the house, along with all the normal hardships of life, mean that most people would say that the Browns are not living the good life. And on their honest days, they admit that it doesn't always seem so good to them either. A few weeks ago Eric posted a photo on Instagram along with a message that read, in part:

> It's been a hard year so far. I'd be lying if I painted it as anything other than a steamroll. Everything that is out of our control (that is to say, everything) seems to be heading the opposite of where we've aimed. Everything we ought to be able to grip just slips through our fingers, and sometimes it seems to do so with a grin. And in spite of my strongest theologies, the lies always seem louder and more believable this time of year. . . . The number of times that I have to stop in a day, zoom out, and try to remind myself of what is true, meaningful, and everlasting is embarrassing. I often praise the idea of weakness, though when weakness moves from theoretical to reality, it can become debilitating rather than romantic.

Sometimes it seems that life just shouldn't be this hard. It can seem that the good life, the life we've always longed for, will always be out of our reach. And there is a bit of truth to that. Something profound shifted in the world when Adam and Eve tried to take hold of the good life in the wrong way rather than trust God to give it to them. That shift left everything a bit off-kilter and some things horribly out of whack. It left us longing for everything to be set right. We long for the good life in which house foundations don't shift, finances are never an issue, relationships are always loving, and bodies are never touched by deformity or disability or death. So is this good life destined to always be out of our reach?

When we read in the first two chapters of the Bible about the way things once were, we see Adam and Eve living together in a perfect environment. Eve had everything she needed and everything she should have wanted—a marriage with no conflict or disappointment and a home decorated by the master designer. Her life had meaning and fruitful purpose. She had no reason to wince when she looked in the mirror, no reason to hide in the presence of God. But she knew there was more. As good as life was in the garden, there was something even better that was to be hers with Adam if they obeyed God.[2] If they passed the probationary test God set before them, the good life they enjoyed in Eden would get even better.[3] Not only would they escape the impact of sin; the possibility of sin would be gone for good. Their life would go from perishable to imperishable, from vulnerable to temptation to impervious to temptation, from the good life to an even better, "unlose-able" life.

In fact, this promise of the better-than-good life, the glorious life, is still held out to you and me. It's there throughout the Bible but made especially clear in its final chapters. At the end of the Bible's story we find the same symbol of this life we long for that was there at the beginning—the tree of life. Here's the promise from Jesus himself: "To the one who conquers I will grant to eat of the tree of life, which is in the paradise of God" (Rev. 2:7). The tree of life is not simply a thing of the past. It's a promise for our future.

The Promise of a Tree in the Garden of Eden

So what is this tree, and can we expect to feast on its fruit? To find out, we have to begin at the very beginning. "And the LORD God planted a garden in Eden, in the east, and there he put the man whom he had formed. And out of the ground the LORD God made to spring up every tree that is pleasant to the sight and good for food" (Gen. 2:8–9).

A garden full of trees—not those ugly, useless scrub trees the builder clears from a lot before building a house. These were lush and verdant trees, beautiful to look at and bearing fruit that tasted delicious. We can almost see the green, feel the shade, taste the juicy fruit, and smell the fragrant aroma of these trees. There was so much goodness for Adam and Eve to relish and enjoy. Among all the trees God planted, two particular trees stood out.

First, there was the tree of life, which was in the midst of the garden (Gen. 2:9). To eat the fruit of this tree would be to enjoy an even better quality of life than what Adam and Eve already enjoyed in Eden. The nourishment this tree offered would satisfy them in a deeper, unending way, leading to an even more secure and glorious life.

It's not that this was a magical tree or that its fruit had some innate power to instill life. Augustine wrote that Adam and Eve "had nourishment in other trees; in this, however, a sacrament."[4] In other words, eating the fruit of this tree would be a symbolic yet edible sign of "the happy life to be passed in paradise and to be changed afterwards into a heavenly life."[5]

It would seem that the fruit of this tree had not yet blossomed, that it was not yet in season. The tree stood in the midst of the garden, with buds preparing to burst into bloom, as a tangible reminder of the promise of the greater life held out to them if they obeyed.[6] We're not told specifically that Adam and Eve could not or did not eat of this tree, but it would seem that eating from this tree was for later, that the fruit of this tree would make a feast for Adam and Eve to eat once they had passed the test of obedience represented in the other tree.[7] The presence of the tree of life communicated to Adam and Eve, "There is even more goodness ahead for you. If you'll trust God to take care of you by obeying his word, you will eat my fruit, and enjoy a life that is even better than the life you enjoy now."

Also in the midst of the garden was the tree of the knowledge of good and evil (Gen. 2:9). We might think that this tree looked evil, that

it was somehow twisted or gave off a foreboding sense o
But there was nothing inherently repulsive or poisonous ꞇ
particular tree. What made it different from all the other tꞇ
what God said about it: "The LORD God commanded the man, ꞇ ꞇ.ng,
'You may surely eat of every tree of the garden, but of the tree of the
knowledge of good and evil you shall not eat, for in the day that you
eat of it you shall surely die'" (Gen. 2:16–17).

What a clear choice—one tree that offers life and another that
threatens death. God intended for Adam and Eve to trust and obey
him regarding this tree, not because they could tell the difference
between this forbidden tree and all the other trees, but simply because he, as their Father, told them to trust and obey him. "It was
not forbidden because it was evil; but evil because it was forbidden."[8] To eat of the tree of the knowledge of good and evil would
not merely enable those who ate it to comprehend good and evil.
To eat of it was to assume the right to decide for oneself what is
good and what is evil rather than depend on God to define good
and evil. This prohibition was essentially a call to faith, a call to
let God be God rather than usurp his authority. Whereas the tree
of life was to be a reward for loyalty, this tree was about to become
a test of loyalty.

Tested by a Tree in the Garden of Eden

Genesis 2:15 tells us, "The LORD God took the man and put him in
the garden of Eden to work it and keep it." In other words, Adam
wasn't just the gardener in the garden; he was to be the guardian of
the garden. When the satanic agent showed up at this tree of judgment, Adam should have guarded the sanctuary of Eden by judging
the Serpent as evil and crushing its head. He should have squashed
this rebellion rather than taking part in it.

The Serpent was cunning but not wise. If he had been wise, he
would have stayed away from the tree where evil is shown to be evil.
Instead, when he slithered up to Eve in the garden, he immediately
focused Eve's attention toward this judgment tree. Rather than stay
away from the forbidden tree, Eve came close to study it. She observed

that the tree looked good. She couldn't see anything about the tree that appeared dangerous or distasteful. The fruit looked delicious. This prohibition didn't make sense to her. And most of us have been there. We don't mind obeying as long as what God has commanded makes sense to us. But when we can't see the harm, when we can't see the problem with whatever it is God has forbidden but instead see something desirable, we can so easily justify doing what we want to do and reach out for what we think we must have.

God had put this tree in the garden as a *test* that would give Adam and Eve the opportunity to live out genuine faith and obedience.[9] But when the Serpent came along, he had his own idea about the tree. He turned the tree into a *temptation* and a *trap*, setting himself up as judge over God's goodness, generosity, and integrity, saying to the woman, "Did God actually say, 'You shall not eat of any tree in the garden'?" (Gen. 3:1).

We can almost hear his tone of voice and see the expression on his scaly serpent face as he not only misrepresented what God had said but cast aspersion on God's character by suggesting that God was unreasonably restrictive. What God had said was that Adam and Eve could eat of every tree in the garden except one. But Eve was open to the Serpent's suggestion of stinginess on God's part. And that causes us to wonder if a sense of resentment regarding this one prohibition has already been simmering inside her. Eve immediately got with the Serpent's program by downplaying the generosity of God as well as exaggerating this singular prohibition. "We may eat of the fruit of the trees in the garden," she said, "but God said, 'You shall not eat of the fruit of the tree that is in the midst of the garden, neither shall you touch it, lest you die'" (Gen. 3:2–3).

She took away the "every" from God's provision and then added the "neither shall you touch it" to his prohibition. Perhaps emboldened by Eve's receptivity, the gloves came off, and the Serpent told Eve that what God had said simply was not so. "You will not surely die," he said (Gen. 3:4).

The Serpent not only said that God was lying to her; he suggested that God was withholding from her. "For God knows that when you eat of it your eyes will be opened, and you will be like God, knowing good and evil" (Gen. 3:5).

There was some truth in this, a partial truth. If they ate of the tree, they would know good and evil. Evil would become a part of them, and good would become a memory of the past. Of course, Adam and Eve could have attained knowledge of good and evil at the tree without eating its fruit. Under the branches of the tree of the knowledge of good and evil, they could have used the wisdom God gave them through his word and judged the Serpent's lies and rebellion against God as evil, while clinging to God's goodness.[10] Had they done so, they would have been able to eat their fill of the tree of life and entered into a heavenly life without ever having to experience death. But instead of trusting in what God said about the tree, Eve listened to what the Serpent told her, which was so very different from what God had said. And as she listened, the tree began to look different.

She began to feel differently about its fruit too. It made sense to her to eat it: it was "good for food." It appealed to her senses: it was "a delight to the eyes." It also appealed to her sense of self: "The tree was to be desired to make one wise" (Gen. 3:6). Who wouldn't want to be wise? The Serpent's words were becoming more believable to her than God's word as she began to think about a wisdom that would become hers by defying rather than fearing God.

The Serpent was successful in his quest to deceive Eve so that she no longer saw the tree as the source of certain death but instead as the source of a happy life. "She took of its fruit and ate, and she also gave some to her husband who was with her, and he ate" (Gen. 3:6). Eve was in search of the good life, and instead of waiting to receive it from the only One who could really provide it, she reached out to take hold of it for herself. Or so she thought.

It sounds so simple, so natural, when in reality it was cosmic and disastrous. Sin is always reckless and foolish. It never makes sense in the light of day. It always takes away rather than adds to our lives. It destroys rather than creates. How we wish Eve had been able to see clearly that in that bite, she was trading blessing for curse, truth for lies, life for death, God as her sovereign for Satan as her slave master. What a terrible trade.

But, of course, we make the same kinds of trades. We trade trusting in God to give us the life that will truly satisfy for grabbing for the life we think will make us happy, only to have the forbidden fruit turn sour in our stomachs. The reason you and I do not have the life we've longed for is not only that Adam and Eve ate of this tree. It's that we put ourselves in the place of God, determining for ourselves what is good and what is evil. We hold grudges against others, deeming ourselves sufficient to determine who does or does not deserve forgiveness. We think our coldness gives them what they deserve, when really our resentment robs us of life. We sleep with someone we're not married to, thinking it is the intimacy we're longing for, only to discover that illicit intimacy isn't enough to satisfy without the security of the lifelong commitment God has prescribed. The intensity of fleeting pleasure is surpassed by the intensity of lingering shame and regret. We're eaten up with anxiety over what is happening or not happening in our lives and the lives of those we love, because we're not sure that God is doing the right thing at the right time. In all these ways and more, we put ourselves in the place of God, determining for ourselves what we deem to be good and evil.

Barred from the Tree in the Garden of Eden

After eating from the tree, Adam and Eve remembered that God had said, "In the day that you eat of it you shall surely die." Today was that day. They didn't die physically, at least not immediately (though one day they would go to earthly graves). They did, however, die spiritually.[11] They went from lives marked by blessing, openness, and intimacy to lives marked by curse, hiding, alienation, and death.

> Then the LORD God said, "Behold, the man has become like one of us in knowing good and evil. Now, lest he reach out his hand and take also of the tree of life and eat, and live forever"—therefore the LORD God sent him out from the garden of Eden to work the ground from which he was taken. He drove out the man, and at the east of the garden of Eden he placed the cherubim and a

flaming sword that turned every way to guard the way to the tree of life. (Gen. 3:22–24)

The way to the tree of life was closed, guarded by two angels with swords—awaiting the offspring of the woman, the coming of the second Adam, the one who would pass through the flaming sword of God's judgment and thereby reopen the way to the tree of life.

Over the centuries that followed, the people of God remembered what was lost even as they waited for the way to the tree of life to be reopened. They were given a pointer toward the way when Moses stood before them as they prepared to enter into the land God had promised to them, which in many ways sounded like a new Eden. Just as Adam and Eve faced a life-or-death choice, a choice between blessing and cursing in the garden, so Israel faced a life-or-death, blessing-or-cursing choice in Canaan. Moses said, "I call heaven and earth to witness against you today, that I have set before you life and death, blessing and curse. Therefore choose life, that you and your offspring may live" (Deut. 30:19).

Along with this encouragement, Israel was also given a picture that would become part of their daily lives to help them see how God's people would one day make their way back to the tree of life. God gave Israel the tabernacle and priests to represent the people in the presence of God. When the high priest went into the holy place in the tabernacle, he was reminded, as he stood before the lampstand, of the fullness of life that was lost in the fall. The lampstand was designed to look like a tree—a golden almond tree with buds, blossoms, almond flowers, and fruit—a reflection of the tree of life.

God also gave his people songs to sing to him. When the people of God sang Psalm 1 about the man who is "like a tree / planted by streams of water / that yields its fruit in its season, / and its leaf does not wither" (v. 3), surely their thoughts went back to the tree of life in the garden, even as singing the song implanted in them a longing to have that kind of life.

When Solomon wrote in Proverbs about the person who finds wisdom, he personified wisdom as having long life in her right hand and "in her left hand are riches and honor. . . . She is a tree of life to those who lay hold of her; / those who hold her fast are called blessed" (Prov. 3:16, 18). It seems that Solomon was reminding God's people that there was still a way to take hold of the fruit of this tree and thereby enjoy the life and blessing it provides.

The prophets also expressed a longing for access to this tree that would bring life and health to a people made sick by sin. One particular prophet, Jeremiah, described his longing for his people in terms of a tree that grew only in Gilead, a region beyond the Jordan River. The resin from this tree, known for its healing properties, was made into a balm that cleansed, soothed, and cured. Because the tree grew only in Gilead, the balm produced from it was costly and precious. Elsewhere Isaiah wrote that God's people were "battered from head to foot—covered with bruises, welts, and infected wounds—without any soothing ointments or bandages" (Isa. 1:6 NLT). Of course, he wasn't talking about physical injuries but about spiritual injuries, self-inflicted wounds caused by sin. Jeremiah didn't want to accept that there was no available cure:

> For the wound of the daughter of my people is my heart
> wounded;
> I mourn, and dismay has taken hold on me.
> Is there no balm in Gilead?
> Is there no physician there?
> Why then has the health of the daughter of my people
> not been restored? (Jer. 8:21–22)

When he asked, "Is there no balm in Gilead?" Jeremiah was expressing his longing for the life and healing God had promised to provide to his people. But, of course, this life and healing would not come from a tree in Gilead. It would come from a tree on Golgotha.

Tested by a Tree in the Garden of Gethsemane

Adam and Eve were tested regarding a tree in a bright and sunny garden where all their needs were met. But Jesus, the second Adam, was tested regarding a tree in the darkness of the garden of Gethsemane. Nothing about this tree of judgment was desirable. He didn't want to eat of it if there was any other way. Yet it was the fruit of this tree that his Father wanted him to eat.

The apostle Peter tells us, "He himself bore our sins in his body on the tree" (1 Pet. 2:24). When Paul described the crucifixion he said, "They took him down from the tree and laid him in a tomb" (Acts 13:29). Why do Peter and Paul call the cross a tree?

Israelites living in Peter and Paul's day would have been familiar with Deuteronomy 21:22–23, which says, "If a man has committed a crime punishable by death and he is put to death, and you hang him on a tree, his body shall not remain all night on the tree, but you shall bury him the same day, for a hanged man is cursed by God." Hanging the body of an offender on a tree was a public sign that having endured the punishment of the people, the offender was now under the curse of God.

This is why Peter and Paul refer to the cross as the tree. When Jesus was crucified at the hands of evil men, he wasn't merely the victim of a miscarriage of human justice; Jesus was under the curse of God. "It was the will of the LORD to crush him; / he has put him to grief" (Isa. 53:10). On that day, human sin, which began at a tree in Eden, was dealt with at another tree, the cross of Calvary.

And here is what we must understand about this tree: I deserve to hang on this tree. You deserve to hang on this tree. But the good news of the gospel is that God "made him to be sin who knew no sin, so that in him we might become the righteousness of God" (2 Cor. 5:21). On this tree, Christ absorbed in himself the full measure of God's wrath so that you and I can experience the full measure of God's blessing. This tree of judgment has become to us a tree of life. Oh, how we bless that cursed tree! When we come under this tree and take hold of its fruit, it changes everything about the story of our lives.

Healed by the Tree in a Garden Better than Eden

Because Jesus hung upon the cursed tree in our place, all who overcome the temptation to grasp for life anywhere other than in him can be sure that there is another tree in our future. We read about it in the last chapter of the last book in the Bible, Revelation 22, where John writes:

> Then the angel showed me the river of the water of life, bright as crystal, flowing from the throne of God and of the Lamb through the middle of the street of the city; also, on either side of the river, the tree of life with its twelve kinds of fruit, yielding its fruit each month. The leaves of the tree were for the healing of the nations. No longer will there be anything accursed, but the throne of God and of the Lamb will be in it, and his servants will worship him. (Rev. 22:1–3)

The scene described by John calls to mind essential features of Eden: the tree of life and the river of life, which, according to Genesis 2:10, flowed out of Eden. In this new Eden, all those whose sin has been dealt with on the tree of Calvary not only drink freely from the river of life; they eat freely from the tree of life. As we look closely, we can't help but recognize that this life-giving, forever-feeding, healing tree is none other than Christ himself.[12] "In him was life" John wrote (John 1:4). And in a sense, this is what Jesus meant during his earthly ministry when he said, "Truly, truly, I say to you, unless you eat the flesh of the Son of Man and drink his blood, you have no life in you. Whoever feeds on my flesh and drinks my blood has eternal life, and I will raise him up on the last day" (John 6:53–54).

Jesus was saying that we must feed on his atoning death as our life. We must see ourselves as we are apart from him, forever cursed, destined for eternal death, unless we become united to him in his death on that tree. Taking and eating what was prohibited by God led to judgment for Adam and Eve, but taking and eating of God's provision of Christ leads to salvation for all who will feast on the fruit of the cross of Christ.

Revelation 22 reveals that the tree of life is gloriously planted in the center of the greater garden to come, which will be more beautiful, more abundant, and more satisfying than the garden of Eden. In Eden, the trees bore fruit in their season, which means once a year. But in the new and better Eden, the tree of life will yield a new crop of fruit every month. In Eden, the tree of life grew in the midst of the garden. But in the new Eden, the tree of life grows on either side of the river. It seems to have multiplied and expanded, implying that everyone will have access to it; all will be welcome to eat their fill.

And it's not just the fruit that will feed us; the leaves of this tree will heal us. In fact, they will heal everything. All the scars left by sin will be healed. All the wounds inflicted by harsh words, the infection of cynical attitudes, the canker sore of racism—it will all be healed. All the emotional scars left by abuse, the relational tearing apart caused by divorce, the societal discord caused by pride, the governmental corruption caused by greed—it will all be healed.

And once this healing happens, doing away with all the sin that led to the sickness, nothing will ever threaten or diminish or disturb our enjoyment of life again. We'll have the life that Eve longed for and foolishly thought she could take hold of by grasping. We'll have it not by grasping for it apart from trusting God to give it to us, but by, in this life, taking hold of Christ, trusting that the life we long for comes only through him.

Do you really believe that the good life comes only through him? Paul did. He said, "For to me to live is Christ, and to die is gain" (Phil. 1:21). To live is not to be married or to have a fulfilling marriage. To live is Christ. To live is not to have children or to raise healthy, successful, or even godly children. To live is Christ. To live is not to have a body of a certain size or shape or degree of health, or a home in a certain neighborhood, or a particular job or status. To live is Christ. And most of us have to be convinced of this today and convinced again tomorrow, because we are so thoroughly immersed in this world that tells us otherwise. This reconvincing happens as we begin eating now of the tree of life by feeding on Christ and his Word today, and again tomorrow, and again the next day.

Recently my friend Eric Brown posted a photo of his wife, Ruth, reading a book to all three of their kids snuggled into Pearl's hospital bed, along with this message:

It was over a fancy breakfast with a dear friend this morning. . . . I was recounting to him my last excursion with such a meal, and how the chef kept bringing out plate after plate for Ruth and [me] to try, and how each time the server brought out a new plate, he would mention that it was compliments of the chef. . . . He stopped me in the middle of my story and cautiously said, "'Compliments of the chef'?! You know that's your whole life story, right? From my perspective—my 30,000-foot flyover perspective of your life—every bit of these last few years has all been compliments of the chef. Do you see that?" And it's true, the Lord has been doubly good to my family. Over and over again, in ways lately I rarely consider, he brings plate after plate out for us, all "compliments of the chef." It's not just Pearl. Or Vandy. Or this house, or this career, or these friends. It includes those things, but it's not primarily those things. It's the joy that always comes back around. It's the peace he gives when the trust he gives prompts the hope he gives to know the strength he gives.

I don't know how long Pearl is going to keep holding onto this life that has been granted to her by the One who gives life. But I do know that Eric and Ruth and Abby and Brennan and Pearl have made their home under the tree of life. And they're not waiting for the next life to experience the healing of its leaves. They're living the good life now as they feed on Christ. It's not the life they expected, probably not the life they would have chosen, but it's good, or, as Eric wrote, "doubly good." It's good now because of the joy and peace and grace that are theirs in Christ as his healing power works its way through their lives and through their perspective about this life. And it's good because of the more complete healing that they know is coming. Perfect healing. Pervasive healing. Permanent healing. Forever healed and whole. The life we all long for.

On a hill far away, stood an old rugged Cross
The emblem of suff'ring and shame
And I love that old Cross where the dearest and best
For a world of lost sinners was slain.

So I'll cherish the old rugged Cross
Till my trophies at last I lay down

I will cling to the old rugged Cross
And exchange it some day for a crown.

To the old rugged Cross, I will ever be true
Its shame and reproach gladly bear
Then He'll call me some day to my home far away
Where his glory forever I'll share.

So I'll cherish the old rugged Cross
Till my trophies at last I lay down
I will cling to the old rugged Cross
And exchange it some day for a crown.[13]

During the editing process of this book, Pearl Joy Brown entered into the joy of her Master. I had the privelege of speaking at her funeral, saying, "What brings the most profound comfort to our grieving hearts is not merely that Pearl is in a better place now; it's that the day is coming when Christ is going to return. Pearl's soul will be with him. He will call Pearl's body out of the grave. She will be completely Pearl, but she will have a radiant glory she didn't have before. Her soul will be reunited with her body, a glorified body fit for living forever with Christ on a glorious new earth."

3

The Story of His Image

These days, if we want to tell someone who we are, we have to be adept at defining it in 160 characters or less. That's all you get to say about who you are in your Twitter bio. For your Instagram bio you get only 150 characters. So how does a person express what is at the heart of who she is in 150 or even 160 characters?

Some people—even dead people and made-up people—find interesting ways to do this. Albert Einstein has a Twitter feed, or more accurately, someone made up a Twitter handle and a bio for him.[1] His Twitter handle is, unsurprisingly, @emc2, and he introduces himself this way: "Former genius, now cartoonish icon representing the word 'smart' in plumbing and used car advertisements." Similarly there is a Twitter account under the name Darth Vader. He uses the handle @darkside. He introduces himself to the Twittersphere this way, "Community Manager

for Sith Lord but tweets are my own. Asthmatic. Dad to two rambunc-
tious Jedis." His website? WhoIsYourDaddy.com. My favorite might be
the Twitter account under the name of "Cowardly Lion," who says about
himself, "Formerly King of the Forest, now Personal Life Coach and Author of *The Courage Trap*. Helping you discover your inner Lion." Likes:
Poppies, Good Witches, Toto. Dislikes: Flying Monkeys, Brooms."

So how about you? When you introduce yourself in person or online, what do you say about who you are and what you do? What does
your introduction say about how you see yourself, about where you
find the source of your identity?

We all struggle with our sense of identity, don't we? (Or is it just me?)
I have a friend in her fifties who's in a bit of an identity crisis, trying to
figure out who she wants to be and what she wants to do when she grows
up. She is one of the most amazing people I know—a godly, radiant,
beautiful, fun person. She's also accomplished a lot in the way that she
has given herself away to her kids and her kids' friends, in the way that
she has given herself away to people around her in times of need, and
the way she has given herself—her credibility, her passion, and plenty of
her money—to a particular cause, all out of love for Christ. But how do
you put those kinds of things on a resume or on a bio that follows your
name on a website? These are the sorts of things that can easily leave us
feeling like nobodies. And, oh, how we long to be somebodies.

I also have friends who have lots of degrees and accomplishments
to go after their names yet still struggle with their sense of identity,
with what has come to define their sense of self. Sometimes we don't
realize how much we've defined ourselves by certain relationships or
roles until those things are taken away from us and we find ourselves
in a full-blown identity crisis.

So how are we meant to see ourselves? And how can finding a
solid source of identity keep us from floundering with a fragile or
distorted sense of self?

Made in the Image of God

In the first chapter of the first book of the Bible we find the foundation stone on which we are meant to build our sense of self. It's found

in Genesis 1:26: "Then God said, 'Let us make man in our image, after our likeness'" (Gen. 1:26). We're reading along in Genesis 1 where the narrator is telling us about all the things that God spoke into being and called "good," and then the language changes. It's not, "Let there be man"; it's, "Let us make man." He's not merely speaking man into existence; the entire Godhead is getting more personally involved. All the animals have been made "according to their kinds," but this particular creation, man, is to be made after God's kind. Evidently God was out to make a creature as much like him as a creature can be. He was out to have a son who looked like him, in fact a people who share his likeness (which, by the way, is still his intention, which will not be thwarted).

But in what way was this creature in his image? We could answer in a number of ways. Some of them come from other places in the Bible that reflect on the creation of man. For example, in Ephesians 4:24 Paul describes being re-created after the likeness of God "in true righteousness and holiness." This tells us that there is an ethical or moral aspect to being made in the image of God. To image God is to do what God would do, and God always does what is right. Paul also speaks of being "renewed in knowledge after the image of its creator" (Col. 3:10). So there is a rational aspect to being made in God's image. To image God is to know what is true and to think the way God thinks.

The psalmist also gives us some insight into what it means to be made in the image of God, when he writes about humanity:

> Yet you have made him a little lower than the heavenly beings
> and crowned him with glory and honor.
> You have given him dominion over the works of your hands;
> you have put all things under his feet. (Ps. 8:5–6)

He is "crowned . . . with glory and honor." To be in the image of God is to be a royal son or daughter. Adam was to be a royal representative of the great King, ruling and exercising dominion in God's holy realm.

If we go back to Genesis 1 we see the same thing that is expressed in Psalm 8: this task of exercising dominion appears to flow out of being made in God's image. We read:

Then God said, "Let us make man in our image, after our likeness. And let them *have dominion* over the fish of the sea and over the birds of the heavens and over the livestock and over all the earth and over every creeping thing that creeps on the earth." (Gen. 1:26)

Image and likeness seem to be connected to exercising dominion, and dominion over something specific. Man made in God's image is supposed to rule over the fish of the sea, birds of the air, and every creeping thing on the earth. (Hmmm. I guess Adam better keep an eye out for creeping things. And he better be ready to rule over that creeping thing instead of allowing it to rule over him.)

So how did being made in God's image impact Adam's sense of self? If you or I met Adam in the garden of Eden and he shook our hand and introduced himself, perhaps he would have said something like this:

Hi, my name is Adam, which means "earth" and also tells you where I came from. God, the great King, formed me from some dust he picked up from the ground. Then he blew his divine breath into me so that I became a living being. Imagine God taking something as ordinary as dust and then infusing it with his own glorious life! God, who is King over everything, made me his royal representative in this holy realm. I'm his vice-regent in the kingdom of Eden. But you could also say I'm the priest in the temple of Eden. I work here in Eden as guardian and gardener. If anything evil or unclean works its way into Eden, it's my job to kill it. And if any rebellion rises up in this garden, it's my job to subdue it. My job is to exercise dominion in God's name, which means that I'm supposed to rule in the way that he rules. He brought order to the formlessness of his creation, and I am to continue bringing order to this garden as well as expand that order into the wilderness outside of the garden. He named the night and the day, the land and the seas, and it's my job to name the livestock and birds and wild animals. (I'm just working my way through the alphabet, and at this point I'm up to baboon, badger, and behemoth.)

I know what you're thinking: I'm going to have to multiply myself to get all this work done. Well, that's part of what I'm supposed to do too. God gave me a helper for all this—woman. She too is made in the image of God, so that means she's royalty too. Together we are going to be fruitful and multiply. We're going to fill this garden with offspring who will be born looking like us but, far more significantly, in the image of God himself. Together we're going to cultivate this garden so that it becomes bigger and more beautiful and will one day cover the whole earth. We're going to develop recipes to make delicious food with this fruit, and we're going to create tools to work in this dirt (which, I've got to say, is very responsive at this point). Together we are going to exercise dominion.

And just so you know, though I've been made in God's image and likeness, there is an even more glorious, enduring, unchanging likeness that is to be mine depending on how I do with all I've been given to do. So there's a chance that if you see me again in the future, you might find it difficult to recognize me, or even look at me, because I'm going to be even more radiant with the glory of God.

What an introduction. What an identity. What a sense of purpose and potential. Oh, how we wish he had fulfilled this purpose and potential.

His Glorious Image Marred

The day came when a particular creeping thing slithered into the garden, and Adam failed to kill it. God's word was twisted and rejected, and Adam failed to correct it. Rebellion rose up in his heart, and Adam failed to subdue it. Righteous judgment was required at the tree, and Adam failed to render it. Instead of ruling over the Serpent, Adam and Eve allowed the Serpent to rule over them.

Adam and Eve, who had been created to rule over creation, became slaves to sin. They went from being crowned with glory and honor to being naked and ashamed.[2] The image of God in them—the image of righteousness, holiness, and knowledge—was marred so that they became corrupt, defiled, and foolish. They still bore God's image, but that image became distorted.[3]

If we had come across Adam as he and Eve headed east from Eden after being cast out of the garden, perhaps he would have introduced himself to us this way:

> Hello, I'm Adam and this is my wife, Eve. We come from Eden, a glorious, abundant, holy place where we were meant to live and enjoy the One who made us and came down to walk with us. We had everything we needed there to fulfill the task that was at the heart of who we were made to be. But we failed. We listened to a creeping thing instead of the Creator. I should have crushed his head instead of letting his crazy ideas fill my head. I should have judged his evil rebellion instead of becoming evil through my own rebellion. I should have protected my wife by affirming what God had said instead of joining my wife in rejecting what God had said.
>
> I'm still a gardener, but the impact of my sin on all of creation means that the job that used to fulfill me now frustrates me. And I'm still a husband, but I'm experiencing a lot of frustration and even some disappointment on that front too. We're still going to be fruitful and multiply, but there will be pain to go with the joy of parenting. And we're still going to live, but we won't live forever like we could have. One day I'm going to die, and they're going to put my body into the ground, and I will turn back into dust— a rather inglorious ending for someone who was made to become glorious, don't you think?
>
> I do want to add this, however: we have hope. I overheard God tell that evil Serpent that one day a child will descend from Eve and me who will crush his head. Evidently he will be the royal son that I wasn't and obey God in the way that I didn't.

His Inglorious Image Reproduced

Genesis 5:3 tells us, "When Adam had lived 130 years, he fathered a son *in his own likeness, after his image,* and named him Seth." Seth was born as a son of Adam with a nature like Adam's. In this way, Adam and Eve filled the earth with offspring who reflected a marred, distorted image of God.

The next time anyone in the Bible is referred to as a son of God comes in Exodus. But this "son" was not a person; it was a nation. Moses was told by God to say to Pharaoh, "Thus says the LORD, Israel is my firstborn son, and I say to you, 'Let *my son* go that he may serve me'" (Ex. 4:22–23). Moses led this "son," the nation of Israel, out of Egypt, across the Red Sea where they camped at the foot of Mount Sinai. God came down on Mount Sinai and, through his mediator Moses, spoke to his people, instilling in them a sense of who they were and what they were to do and not do. It sounded like this:

> You yourselves have seen what I did to the Egyptians, and how I bore you on eagles' wings and brought you to myself. Now therefore, if you will indeed obey my voice and keep my covenant, you shall be my treasured possession among all peoples, for all the earth is mine; and you shall be to me a kingdom of priests and a holy nation. (Ex. 19:4–6).

If you had met one of these Israelites camped at the foot of this mountain, she might have said something like:

> Hi. I'm Elisheba, the daughter of Amminadab and the sister of Nahshon, the wife of Aaron, who is Moses's brother and soon-to-be high priest. And I'm having a bit of an identity crisis. Up to this point in my life I've been a slave. It's all I've known. Certainly I heard about Yahweh, who made so many promises to our ancestor, Abraham, but, honestly, after four hundred years of slavery and silence, I didn't know if Yahweh even saw what was happening to us or if he heard our cries or cared. But then he sent Moses back to Egypt to bring us out, and now Yahweh is here in the wilderness *with* us. He covers us in a glorious cloud during the hot days and as a pillar of fire at night. He has told us that we are to be a kingdom of priests—that we are going to represent him to all the nations of the earth. He said we are a holy nation. We've been set apart from all the other nations of the earth to be—get this—his treasured possession. Now, I brought a few treasured possessions with me out of Egypt. They are valuable and precious to me, and I protect them. So I'm trying to let it sink in that that is what we are to Yahweh.

In light of who they were and in response to the grace shown to them, God made clear what they were to do and not do:

> I am the LORD your God, who brought you out of the land of Egypt, out of the house of slavery. You shall have no other gods before me. You shall not make for yourself a carved image, or any likeness of anything that is in heaven above, or that is in the earth beneath, or that is in the water under the earth. You shall not bow down to them or serve them. (Ex. 20:2–5)

So after hearing Moses read through these commands, Elisheba might have wanted to add:

> Because of who we are—a people who belong to God, are treasured by God, and are headed to live in a new land with God—God has told us what it should look like for us to live our lives with a rich sense of this identity. And the number-one thing this means is that Yahweh will be our one and only God. We're not going to worship any of the gods they worshiped in Egypt or the gods that the people worship where we're headed in Canaan. God has loved us so much; we want to love and serve him exclusively in return.
>
> The way we worship God is going to be very different from the way all the other peoples of the earth worship their gods. We are not to make an image of him to worship. The Creator God can't be reduced to any one thing in creation. Besides, God has already made images of himself—us! We are to image God in the world!

Elisheba seemed to understand what God was saying about himself and about his people. But she and her husband, Aaron, and the rest of Israel evidently did not let this reality change them at the core of who they were.

In the Image of Other Gods

Before Moses could get down from the mountain with all that God told him about who Israel was to be and how the people were to live in the world as his representatives, the people had pitched all their gold into a fire, and Aaron had formed it into the image of a calf. In recording the story, Moses seems to want us to see that we always resemble what we revere, that we come to look like whatever we worship.[4] Clearly that was the case for the Israelites. After this incident Moses describes the Israelites as "stiff-necked," as those who had been "let loose" and needed to be "gathered together" again in the gate so that Moses could lead them where they needed to go,[5] which sounds like how you'd describe a herd of cattle, doesn't it?

After the Israelites settled in the land God gave them, they refused to see themselves as one-God people but instead bowed down to all kinds of pagan gods. The prophet Isaiah used his pulpit and pen to make fun of the stupidity of it all. He wrote about how ridiculous it is for a person to plant a tree, harvest it, and then carve it into a god to bow down to:

> Half of it he burns in the fire. Over the half he eats meat; he roasts it and is satisfied. Also he warms himself and says, "Aha, I am warm, I have seen the fire!" And the rest of it he makes into a god, his idol, and falls down to it and worships it. He prays to it and says, "Deliver me, for you are my god!" (Isa. 44:16–17)

God spoke to his people through the prophets, calling them to forsake their idols. "But they would not listen, but were stubborn, as their fathers had been, who did not believe in the LORD their God. They despised his statutes and his covenant that he made with their fathers and the warnings that he gave them. They went after false idols and became false, and they followed the nations that were around them" (2 Kings 17:14–15). What a sad state of affairs for a people who had been given such a grand purpose and identity. It took seventy years of exile in Babylon to purge his people of their idols.

His Glorious Image Incarnate

Then, finally, the image of the invisible God, the One in whom all the fullness of God was pleased to dwell (Col. 1:15, 19), condescended to live among those made in God's image. God sent his Son, wrapped in human flesh, into the world. John begins his Gospel saying about Jesus, "No one has ever seen God; the only God, who is at the Father's side, he has made him known" (John 1:18). While Adam was created *in* the image of God, Jesus *is* the image of God par excellence. He is not simply a reflection of the image of God but is the origin and source, the Alpha and the Omega, the one from whom we draw our image and the target toward which the image of God in us is being restored. "He is the radiance of the glory of God and the exact imprint of his nature" (Heb. 1:3).

Have you ever wondered how Jesus's sense of self was shaped as he grew? It came from reading the scrolls that contained the writings of Moses and the Prophets. There he "found the shape of his own identity and goal of his own mission."[6] As he grew in his understanding of the Scriptures, his sense of himself as the Son of God developed. It also became clear to his earthly parents when Jesus lingered at the temple and responded to their worried search for him by saying, "Why were you looking for me? Did you not know that I must be in my Father's house?" (Luke 2:49). This sense of identity drove his sense of mission. He said, "I came from God and I am here. I came not of my own accord, but he sent me. . . . I came that they may have life and have it abundantly" (John 8:42; 10:10). Of course he also said, "For judgment I came into this world" (John 9:39).

If John had created a Twitter handle for Jesus, perhaps it would have been: @beforeAbrahamwasIAM. And maybe John would have written his bio this way: "Bread of life. Light of the world. Door of the sheep. Good shepherd. True vine. Resurrection and the life. Way, truth, life."

If Paul had created a Twitter handle for Jesus, perhaps it would have been: @firstbornofallcreation. And maybe Paul would have written his bio this way: "Image of the invisible God, Creator. Before all things. Over all things. Head of the body, the church. Reconciler. Peacemaker. Cross carrier. Ultimate overcomer."

And if the writer of Hebrews had created a Twitter handle for Jesus, perhaps it would have been simply: @better. And maybe his bio would have read: "God created all things through me and has appointed me as heir of all things. I am the radiance of the glory of God, the exact imprint of his nature, and I uphold the universe by the word of my power. #betterthanMoses #betterpriest #bettersacrifice #bettermediator #bettercountry."

In the earthly ministry of Jesus we see him doing what the first Adam should have done. Adam was supposed to exercise dominion. Jesus exercised dominion over demons, over nature, over sickness, and even over death. By taking upon himself a human nature, and living in that human nature in true righteousness and holiness, Jesus demonstrated for us what it means to be truly and fully human.

But he did more than that. He made it possible for the image of God to be restored in us. How? He who bore the perfect image became marred—not by his own sin but by ours. Isaiah wrote, "His appearance was so marred, beyond human semblance, / and his form beyond that of the children of mankind" (Isa. 52:14). On the cross, our King—the One who was perfect in righteousness, holiness, and knowledge—took upon himself all our rebellion, our filthiness, our foolishness. The One who is life itself entered into death.

But he didn't stay there. When Jesus emerged from the grave, he didn't look like he'd looked before. Those who had been closest to him didn't recognize him. He was still human; the first glorified human. But he won't be the last! The Father intends for the Son to have many brothers and sisters and for the whole family to look like him, to be glorious like the risen Jesus!

You see, when we read in Romans 8:29 that "those whom he foreknew he also predestined to be conformed to the image of his Son, in order that he might be the firstborn among many brothers," we recognize that it has always been God's plan to have the earth filled with his image bearers, with people who look like him. But we have to ask ourselves: Which image? Is it God's intention that we would look like Adam and Eve did in Eden before the fall? No! God intends for us to bear his image far more intensely, far more securely, far more permanently and pervasively than Adam and Eve bore that image in Eden. Does he intend for us to look like Jesus during his life and ministry? Certainly Jesus provides a model for us in his righteous life. But God intends for us to bear his image far more openly and radiantly than Jesus did in his life and ministry. God intends for us to bear the image of the risen and glorified Jesus! "Just as we have borne the image of the man of dust, we shall also bear the image of the man of heaven" (1 Cor. 15:49). And he's not waiting until resurrection day to get started on this lifelong process of image and identity transformation.

His Glorious Image Renewed

If you have been joined to Christ by faith, the process of your being remade into the image of the resurrected Christ has already begun. How do we know that? Paul says that we are those "on whom the end of the ages has come" (1 Cor. 10:11). The new is breaking into the now. We aren't yet *totally* new, but we are *genuinely* new.[7] "He who has prepared us for this very thing is God, who has given us the Spirit as a guarantee" (2 Cor. 5:5). In the vocabulary of Peter, we've become "partakers of the divine nature" (2 Pet. 1:4).

This means that even now, as you and I are joined to Christ by faith, we "have put on the new self, which *is being renewed* in knowledge after the image of its creator" (Col. 3:10). We've "put on the new self, created after the likeness of God in true righteousness and holiness" (Eph. 4:24). As we abide in Christ and saturate our hearts and minds with the Scriptures, and as we welcome the convicting, cleansing work of the Spirit in our lives, what the Scriptures say about who we are is beginning to shape our sense of self more than what the mirror or the culture around us or even our own bio says about us. This means we can introduce ourselves this way:

> Hi, I'm Nancy. I live here in Nashville for now, but this is just temporary. My real citizenship is in heaven. And I am not alone in this. I'm part of a family. I am a fellow citizen with the saints and members of the household of God. We are a part of the people of God that spans the centuries and reaches even into the ancient church, which means that we are a chosen race, a royal priesthood, a holy nation, a people for God's own possession. And we've been given a great commission—to proclaim the excellencies of him who called us out of darkness into his marvelous light.

Because I've become joined to Christ by faith, I've been raised with Christ. I'm seeking the things that are above, where Christ is, seated at the right hand of God. If it seems like I don't get all worked up about getting attention or advancement or affirmation here and now, it's because I've set my mind on things above, not on things on earth. And if it seems strange that I'm not afraid of losing out here or even afraid of losing my life, it's because I've already died, and my life is hidden with Christ in God. And when Christ, who is my life, appears, I'm going to appear with him in glory.[8]

His Glorious Image Revealed

My friends, God, by his Spirit, is at work restoring his likeness in you, the way it once was in Eden, except even better.[9] Adam and Eve gave their allegiance to the Serpent instead of God. But when the image of God is fully restored in you, affection for and adoration of God will consume you. Old ways of always thinking of yourself first will be gone for good so that you will finally be able to love God and others in sincerity, purity, and harmony.

If you are in Christ, you will be part of a kingdom and priests to our God and will reign on the earth (Rev. 5:10). Because you will have been made holy through and through, you won't be tempted to dominate or oppress or abuse or exploit. Your rule with Christ over the new creation will look just like your heavenly Father's rule over all things—perfect in righteousness and justice.

The day is coming when people will know who you are just by looking at you. You won't even have to introduce yourself. They'll see that you are all you were meant to be and that you are doing all you were meant to do. Your face will radiate the glory of God himself, and your days will be filled with ruling over all he has made. Your heart and motives will be perfectly pure. Your thoughts and actions will be completely wise. They're going to say that you look like your heavenly Father, that you have a strong resemblance to your heavenly brother, and that clearly the Spirit's work in you is complete—you've been fully remade in the image of God. But if you do want to introduce yourself, it might sound something like this:

I could give you the name my parents gave to me when I was born on the old earth under the old order, but that name simply doesn't define me anymore. I'm still me, but my identity is now so thoroughly defined by Christ that my old name just doesn't seem able to communicate who I am.[10] What a relief to be fully myself, yet not full of myself.

I've got to tell you that I wish I could talk to my old self, back when I was living under the old order. I would want to tell the earthbound me to look up, look ahead! You think your life is defined by the body you see when you look in the mirror, and the job you have or don't have, or by the titles after your name. But they don't. Who you are is most profoundly about who Christ is and who the Spirit is making you to be. Your sense of identity is being shaped by your sense of being made in his image. But more than that, it is being shaped by your anticipation of being remade in his glorious image!

On the days when you are doing the lowliest of tasks, on the days when you feel invisible and insignificant, on the days when you compare yourself to everyone around you who seems to be doing far more significant things with their lives, take stock of who you really are, because you are united to Christ, the King. When you know that you are seated with him in heavenly places, you will be able to lower yourself to do the most menial tasks and go to the most needful of places to give yourself away. When you know that the righteousness of Christ defines you now and into eternity, shame over your sin won't have the power to shape how you see yourself.

Remember how Paul wrote that "in the coming ages" God intended to "show the immeasurable riches of his grace in kindness toward us in Christ Jesus" (Eph. 2:7)? I've got to go now because the show is starting.[11] But you can follow me on Twitter. Just look for my bio, which reads: "Redeemed, righteous, royal inhabitant of heaven. Foreknown. Predestined to be and now fully conformed to the image of Christ. Called. Justified. Glorified. #nomoretears #myfuturessobrightIgottawearshades #thisiswaybetterthanEden."

Have Thine own way, Lord! Have Thine own way!
Thou art the Potter, I am the clay.
Mold me and make me after Thy will,
While I am waiting, yielded and still.

Have Thine own way, Lord! Have Thine own way!
Hold o'er my being absolute sway!
Fill with Thy Spirit till all shall see
Christ only, always, living in me.[12]

4

The Story of Clothing

I hate to be typical. But I must admit that I am relieved to know that some of my recurring dreams are actually very typical. Evidently I'm not the only person who sometimes has dreams in which I can fly without the assistance of an airplane as well as dreams in which I'm out in public with no shirt on. (You've had those too, right?) According to a study conducted at the University of California Santa Cruz,[1] the two most frequently reported recurring dreams are what they call "inappropriate dress" dreams—those in which you are wearing no clothes or the completely wrong clothes—and flying dreams—those in which you are effortlessly able to fly. I've had plenty of both. What's interesting is that people in the study weren't bothered by the dreams in which they were able to fly. There's something pleasant and empowering about that dream. But people found the dreams in which they were under- or inappropriately dressed significantly troubling. Isn't our familiarity with this anxiety the reason we call our friends to ask what they are wearing to a particular event? We don't want to show up dressed inadequately, or all wrong.

When I was a senior in high school, I went to Girls State, which ended with a banquet at which each girl had to walk across the stage and give her name. I had bought a special dress for the event, or so I thought. I ordered it from the Spiegel catalog for thirty-two dollars (this was 1979, mind you, and that was big money for me). Evidently some other girls had the same bright idea. Six—count them—six other girls paraded past me with the very same "special" dress, and we awkwardly smiled and rolled our eyes at each other.

Nobody likes being inappropriately or inadequately dressed. I can't help but wonder if this recurring dream about clothes emerges not only from our anxiety over the possibility of being exposed and embarrassed, but also from a deeper place in our ancestral memory— a sense of shame and the accompanying anxiety produced by our inability to find appropriate cover, a shame we inherited from our common parents, Adam and Eve.

Adam and Eve's state of physical undress in Eden wasn't at all troubling at first. Moses writes in Genesis 2:25, "The man and his wife were both naked and were not ashamed." They were, after all, made in the image of God, whom the psalmist says is "clothed with splendor and majesty, / covering [him]self with light as with a garment" (Ps. 104:1–2). If they were made in God's image, they must have had some of this same splendor and majesty as a covering. David wrote about the first man, "You have made him a little lower than the heavenly beings / and crowned him with glory and honor" (Ps. 8:5). When Adam and Eve looked at each other, or at their own reflection, they would have seen themselves covered with a measure or degree of the radiant light of the righteousness, beauty, and glory of God, which is why there was no cause for shame.[2]

But that doesn't mean there was no need for further clothing. When Moses writes that Adam and Eve were naked, his ancient Near Eastern readers would have recognized this as an undesirable condition for human beings, particularly for royal representatives.³ Adam and Eve were representatives of the great King, and royal representatives should dress the part. (Consider Joseph's coat of many colors, Jonathan giving David his royal robe acknowledging he would be the next king, Daniel being given a purple robe by Belshazzar when proclaimed the third-highest ruler in the kingdom and the prodigal son being given a robe upon his return.⁴) We might think of being naked and unashamed as wonderfully freeing, but by stating that Adam and Eve were naked, it's as if Moses intended to prompt some questions in the minds of his readers—not so much *whether* Adam and Eve would be clothed, but *how* and *when* they would be clothed. *Would Adam and Eve obey and trust that God would clothe them as royalty, or would they seek to clothe themselves? Would they remain free of shame, or would something transpire to cause them great shame?*

The Possibility of Being Clothed

When I say that Moses presents Adam and Eve as naked and needing to be clothed, perhaps you think I'm suggesting that paradise was somehow imperfect. But perfect or imperfect probably isn't the right way to seek to define Eden. Certainly Eden was pure and pristine, ordered and filled and, as God himself said, good, and even very good. But rather than thinking of Eden in terms of perfection, we should think of it in terms of potential. Or, as my friend Buz Graham put it recently, "Eden was unspoiled but also unfinished."

In Genesis 1 and 2 we're reading the beginning of a story that will be interrupted and rerouted when it has barely gotten started. God's original intention for Eden was that it be not just good, but glorious. Likewise, God's original intention for Adam and Eve was that they would be transformed into a fuller, more complete likeness of God by being clothed in a greater measure of the beauty and glory of God. They were to go from glory to greater glory, from being clothed with life in Eden to being clothed with immortality in a bigger and better Eden. As Adam and Eve were fruitful and multiplied, more offspring in the image of God would come to glorify God and enjoy him forever. As Adam and Eve worked and kept the garden, Eden would grow beyond its current boundaries, and the glory of their royal rule would increase. If Adam and Eve had obeyed God's command regarding the forbidden tree, they would have been transformed from glory to glory, from a state of untested righteousness to that of tested and confirmed righteousness.[5] They would have been fully and forever clothed with a holiness that would never be sullied, a beauty that would never become marred, and a glory that would never fade.

But, of course, we know that is not what happened. They fell short of the glory of God, the glory God intended for them. In eating from the tree, Adam and Eve sought to become like God, to be dressed in the beauty and glory of God, apart from God. And instantly, instead of reflecting the image of their Creator, they began to reflect the image of their new god, the ancient Serpent. And it was ugly, unbearable, shameful.

And then came the rumble of footsteps in the garden. The Lord's warning—that in the day they ate of the tree of the knowledge of good and evil, they would die—must have thundered in their ears. Today was that day. What they heard was not the gentle footsteps of a friend but the threatening footsteps of a judge. They understood that the worst possible scenario for a sinner is to be found in a state of undress before God, so they scrambled to make clothing for themselves by sewing together some leaves. What a sad state of affairs. They were meant to be clothed by God in the royal garments of his righteousness and glory, and the best they could do was clothe themselves in leaves from the fig tree in the backyard.

And the fig leaves just didn't do the job. Have you ever worn something that didn't quite fit right and didn't cover everything that needed to be covered? When that happens, you find yourself self-consciously tugging at your clothes, trying to keep certain skin from showing. I imagine Adam and Eve self-consciously tugging at these leaves that were clearly inadequate. They were trying to keep their shame from showing. Their uncomfortable, inadequate, self-styled solution to shame clearly wasn't working. So they hid from God.

When we see Adam tell God why he is hiding, we might expect that he'd say it's because he ate the fruit of the forbidden tree. But that's not what he says. Instead he explains, "I was afraid, *because I was naked*, and I hid myself" (Gen. 3:10). His fear was based in his awareness of the loss of his original likeness to the righteous and glorious God, which granted him the right to be in God's presence.[6]

So what did God do? Instead of destroying Adam and Eve, God clothed them. "And the LORD God made for Adam and for his wife garments of skins and clothed them" (Gen. 3:21). It wasn't the way they would have been clothed had they obeyed, but it did provide some protection from the harsh wilderness they would encounter outside of Eden. It also hinted that the possibility of being clothed by God in holiness, beauty, and glory was not gone forever.[7] In fact, in clothing them with the skins of an innocent animal, God demonstrated *how* it would be possible for his people to one day be clothed in the royal splendor he had intended for Adam and Eve. One day he would deal with human sin in a pervasive and permanent way—through the covering provided by the atoning death of one precious, perfect Lamb. One day, in the better Eden to come, he would clothe his people in robes washed white by the blood of this Lamb (Rev. 7:14).

The Preview of Being Clothed

Adam and Eve were meant to rule as royalty over the kingdom of Eden. They were also to serve as priests in the cosmic temple of Eden. Had they passed the test of the tree, God would have clothed them in garments appropriate for this priestly duty. But the failure of Adam and Eve did not frustrate God's plan. Instead, he began working out his plan in which a representative of his people would enter into his presence in the Most Holy Place of the tabernacle, and later the temple, once a year. God gave Moses divine designs for the temple, and particularly the Most Holy Place, which would make it reminiscent of Eden. He also stipulated the design for the clothing of the high priest. In the divine design of the high priest's clothing, we get a sense not only of how Adam and Eve would have been clothed had they obeyed, but also how God intends to clothe all who will one day inhabit the sanctuary that is better than Eden, those "from every tribe and language and people and nation" whom God has made "a kingdom and priests to our God" who will "reign on the earth" (Rev. 5:9–10).

God's instruction to Moses was, "You shall make *holy* garments for Aaron your brother, for *glory* and for *beauty*" (Ex. 28:2). Those three words capture the distinctiveness of the high priest's clothing: *holy*, *glory*, and *beauty*. He was to be the best-dressed man in Israel, in robes made of pure white linen decorated with gold, blue, purple, and scarlet yarn.

He wore an ephod, which was likely a long, sleeveless apron or vest with two straps that went over his shoulders. There were two semiprecious stones mounted on the shoulder straps, which were inscribed with the names of the twelve tribes of Israel. Attached to the front of the ephod was a fabric breastpiece with twelve precious stones mounted on it, one for each of the twelve tribes. The high priest also wore a robe made of blue or violet, a seamless garment that went under the ephod and hung down to the knees. He wore a turban of fine linen with a gold plate affixed to the front engraved with the words "Holy to the Lord," signifying that he, and the people that he represented before God, were set apart by God and to God to be a holy nation.[8]

Holy—out of the ordinary, intended for special use by God. *Beautiful*—not seductive or sexy, but beautiful in its truest sense, with symmetry and perfection that reflected God's own beauty and perfections. *Glorious*—a radiant expression of all that God is and does. Who would not want to be clothed this way?

Over the centuries plenty of priests were clothed this way. But the outer clothing simply didn't have the power to change the inner person. As we read through the history of Israel in the Old Testament, we discover that, as much as anything else, it was the corruption of the priests that led Israel into exile, and eventually the priesthood broke down altogether. The day came when there was no priest wearing the ephod to represent the people of God in the temple in Jerusalem. In fact, there was no temple in Jerusalem.

The Promise of Being Clothed

But there was hope offered by the prophet Isaiah. Isaiah spoke of a servant of the Lord who would come, one who would give his people "a beautiful headdress instead of ashes, / the oil of gladness instead of mourning, / the garment of praise instead of a faint spirit" (Isa. 61:3). God's people would "be called the priests of the Lord" (Isa. 61:6). In Isaiah's prophesy we hear the servant speaking. He's celebrating:

> I will greatly rejoice in the LORD;
>> my soul shall exult in my God,
> for he has clothed me with the garments of salvation;
>> he has covered me with the robe of righteousness,
> as a bridegroom decks himself like a priest with a beautiful
>> headdress,
> and as a bride adorns herself with her jewels. (Isa. 61:10)

The day was coming when God's people would be clothed with salvation, covered with righteousness, and beautifully dressed like a priest. But when? And how?

That hope of being clothed—pictured in the clothing of skins made for Adam and Eve and in the clothing of the high priest, and promised by the prophets—was becoming a reality when Mary "gave birth to her firstborn son and wrapped him in swaddling cloths" (Luke 2:7). "He had no form or majesty that we should look at him, / and no beauty that we should desire him" (Isa. 53:2). Why couldn't we see his beauty? Because "though he was in the form of God, [he] did not count equality with God a thing to be grasped, but emptied himself, by taking the form of a servant, being born in the likeness of men" (Phil. 2:6–7). Jesus clothed himself in the ordinary, perishable clothing of human flesh.

There was, however, one day when he gave a few of his followers a glimpse of his true beauty, his glorious clothing. Mark tells us, "Jesus took with him Peter and James and John, and led them up a high mountain by themselves. And he was transfigured before them, and his clothes became radiant, intensely white, as no one on earth could bleach them" (Mark 9:2–3). Peter, James, and John got a preview of the resurrection glory of Jesus. But it wasn't just a preview of Jesus's resurrection glory. It was a preview of the resurrection glory of all who are joined to Jesus by faith. "Our citizenship is in heaven, and from it we await a Savior, the Lord Jesus Christ, who will transform our lowly body to be like his glorious body" (Phil. 3:20–21). One day we're going to be clothed with the same glory that radiated from Jesus on that mountain. We're going to be that radiant; we're going to be that beautiful.

The Priest Who Was Stripped of Clothes

To make it possible for you and me to be clothed in this way, Jesus submitted himself not only to being born as a naked baby but also to being stripped naked in his crucifixion. John tells us:

> When the soldiers had crucified Jesus, they took his garments and divided them into four parts, one part for each soldier; also his tunic. But the tunic was seamless, woven in one piece from top to bottom, so they said to one another, "Let us not tear it, but cast lots for it to see whose it shall be." This was to fulfill the Scripture which says,
>
> > "They divided my garments among them,
> > and for my clothing they cast lots." (John 19:23–24)

Jesus, wearing the seamless garment of a priest, was stripped of that garment. He experienced the humiliation of nakedness so that you and I can experience the glory of being clothed. And this isn't relegated solely to the future. Right now, if you are in Christ, you are being made holy, you are becoming beautiful, you are being clothed in the righteousness of Christ.

The Process of Becoming Clothed

In the book of Colossians, Paul speaks to believers about the impact of having been joined to Christ. He writes:

> If then you have been raised with Christ, seek the things that are above, where Christ is, seated at the right hand of God. Set your minds on things that are above, not on things that are on earth. For you have died, and your life is hidden with Christ in God.

When Christ who is your life appears, then you also will appear with him in glory. (Col. 3:1–4)

In other words, because you are joined to Christ, the new-creation reality of resurrection is already yours. The day is coming when you will be fully clothed in the glory of Jesus. So it only makes sense that his glory—his character, his purpose, his likeness—would become an increasing reality in what you're "wearing" now, the way you're living now.

Paul tells believers that because we are hidden in or covered in Christ, we "have put off the old self with its practices and have put on the new self, which is being renewed in knowledge after the image of its creator" (Col. 3:9–10). It is almost as if Paul has Genesis 1–3 in mind as he writes. He's saying that we have taken off the clothing that all who are "in Adam" wear—the covering of rebellion and the fig leaves of our own attempts to be good enough to be in the presence of God—and now we have put on this "new self." Now we are wearing the clothing of the last Adam, Christ Jesus.[9]

And what does this new clothing look like? Paul continues:

Put on then, as God's chosen ones, holy and beloved, compassionate hearts, kindness, humility, meekness, and patience, bearing with one another and, if one has a complaint against another, forgiving each other; as the Lord has forgiven you, so you also must forgive. And above all these put on love, which binds everything together in perfect harmony. (Col. 3:12–14)

This, my friends, is what it means to be beautiful. This is the "imperishable beauty of a gentle and quiet spirit, which in God's sight is very precious" (1 Pet. 3:4). Not only is this beautiful to God; it's pretty appealing to people too.

Paul is saying that as the new creation breaks into the here and now of our lives, it only makes sense that we would be increasingly covered in the holiness, glory, and beauty that will one day be ours in full. And that's what Paul says is happening in 2 Corinthians 3. He recalls how Moses would come out of the presence of God with the glory of God covering his face and would put a veil over it so that others wouldn't see the glory fading away. He's helping us to understand that there are degrees of glory that can increase and decrease. The glory Moses had on his face when he came out of God's presence would decrease over time. Paul says, "We all, with unveiled face, beholding the glory of the Lord, are being transformed into the same image from one degree of glory to another" (v. 18). The glory you and I have is meant to increase over the course of our lives.

"Transformed from one degree of glory to another"—that has always been God's plan. That was his plan for Adam and Eve. Adam and Eve were created with a degree of glory, having been made in the image of God. Had they obeyed, they would have been transformed from that first degree of glory to another. But they failed. Christ has made it possible for us to actually be clothed in the greater glory Adam and Eve forfeited. Even now, as the Holy Spirit works in us, we are being changed from one degree of glory to another.

As we bring ourselves naked and exposed before the Word of God, this living and active Word goes to work in the interior of our lives, discerning our impure thoughts and ugly intentions of the heart so that we can confess, repent, and truly change (Heb. 4:12–13). The Spirit does his work of transformation so that we are increasingly wrapped in the robes of the righteousness of Christ—not simply in a judicial sense, but in the reality of our lives.

The Spirit empowers us to leave behind our rebellious determination to flaunt our shameful sinfulness, and our self-righteous determination to clothe ourselves in our own glory, righteousness, and beauty. We find ourselves increasingly wanting to be clothed in the glory, holiness, and beauty of Christ himself. We want to "put on the Lord Jesus Christ, and make no provision for the flesh, to gratify its desires" (Rom. 13:14). We want to put on the "new self, created after the likeness of God in true righteousness and holiness" (Eph. 4:24). We want to put on the whole armor of God (Eph. 6:11–15). What a wardrobe! Who needs Nordstrom? When we put our focus on being clothed in this way, we become less invested and anxious about how we look in our physical clothes. We know that if the One who is clothing the lilies of the field is the same One clothing us, we can only begin to imagine how beautiful we're becoming.

Because the Spirit is at work in us changing how we think about nakedness and clothing, rather than being casual about nudity, we see the nudity of others and our viewing of it, or joining in it, as shameful rebellion against God, as a denial of our sinfulness before a holy God. We embrace modesty rather than exposure. Every day when we cover ourselves with clothing, we bear witness to our past and present failure, which brings shame, but also to the glory that will cover us for all eternity and eradicate all shame.

The Spirit at work in us is replacing our desire to dress in a way that impresses or seduces with a desire to dress as Paul instructed women in his letter to Timothy, "in respectable apparel, with modesty and self-control" (1 Tim. 2:9). Rather than making a fashion statement with our clothes that will cause heads to turn in our direction, we want to make a fashion statement with our character that will cause heads to turn in Christ's direction. We want others to look at our lives and ask where we got our outfit because they want to become as beautiful as we're becoming.

The Anticipation of Being Further Clothed

We relish the way God is clothing us now in holiness, beauty, and glory. But we also recognize that we are not nearly as holy, as beautiful, or as glorious as we long to be. This is what Paul is getting at when he writes to the Corinthians that we groan even as we long to be "further clothed" (2 Cor. 5:4). To follow what Paul is saying in this passage, we have to recognize that he mixes two metaphors—that of a building we live in and of clothing we're wearing. They refer to the same thing. Paul writes:

> For we know that if the tent that is our earthly home is destroyed, we have a building from God, a house not made with hands, eternal in the heavens. For in this tent we groan, longing to put on our heavenly dwelling, if indeed by putting it on we may not be found naked. For while we are still in this tent, we groan, being burdened—not that we would be unclothed, but that we would

be further clothed, so that what is mortal may be swallowed up by life. (2 Cor. 5:1–4)

Paul describes the present life as living in a tent, which is temporary and vulnerable. And he describes our life in the future both as "putting on" a heavenly dwelling and as being "further clothed." He doesn't want to be "found naked." Evidently the glory with which we will be clothed at the resurrection is going to be so much greater than the glory with which we are covered now that our current reality can be described by contrast only as nakedness.[10] Why do we want to be "further clothed"? "So that what is mortal may be swallowed up by life." In other words, we long to be further clothed with immortality.

If we've read Paul's earlier letter to the Corinthians, this sounds familiar. In 1 Corinthians 15 Paul says that the glory we'll have when we are raised from the dead is going to be so much greater than the glory we have now, that our current state can be described only as "dishonor" in comparison.[11] Then he describes the day when we will get the wardrobe we've longed for: "The trumpet will sound, and the dead will be raised imperishable, and we shall be changed. For this perishable body must *put on* the imperishable, and this mortal body must *put on* immortality" (vv. 52–53).

This will be the ultimate outfit: immortality. Unending, unstoppable life. You can't order it from the Spiegel catalog, and it costs a whole lot more than thirty-two dollars. But *you* can't buy it; it has to be purchased *for* you, and in fact it has been purchased for you. "You were ransomed from the futile ways inherited from your forefathers, not with perishable things such as silver or gold, but with the precious blood of Christ" (1 Pet. 1:18–19). For all eternity you're going to be wearing the most expensive outfit ever.

I love the imagery Paul uses of mortality being swallowed up by life—overcome, chewed up, by it. Our mortality, which sometimes causes us such angst, is going to be swallowed up by life. Just think of all the ways the world tries to sell us a counterfeit version of immortality in the form of plastic surgery and Botox and hair coloring and wrinkle creams. Think of all the ways we obsess about becoming and looking older. Here is just one place where saturating our thinking with the Bible's story changes us in the here and now. As the certainty of our immortality begins to take root in our souls, it has the power to keep us from feeling so desperate as our youth slips away. We can rest, knowing that we are going to be clothed in holiness and beauty and glory forever. This is the clothing we want for ourselves and for everyone we love.

When I was pregnant with my daughter, Hope, my friend Dee Proctor hosted a shower for me. Among the many beautiful things I received at that shower was a nine-month-size bunting from Jan Eberle, purchased from one of the nicest children's clothing stores in Nashville. When Hope was born a few weeks later, we learned that her life would be very short. The geneticist told us to expect that we would have her for about six months.[12] A couple of months into her life, we were preparing for a special occasion, and I wanted to dress Hope in something especially beautiful. So I took that nine-month-size bunting back to the store and asked if I could trade it for something else. The sweet woman working in the store said, "Oh, but don't you want to keep this for when she grows into it this winter?" I had to tell her that Hope was not going to live into the coming winter (the kind of awkward conversation I had many times during Hope's brief life). I came away from the store with a beautiful smocked gown, and she wore it the next day. Then a few months later, when Hope died, and I handed over her body, the mortician asked if I had a particular outfit I wanted Hope to be buried in, and I gave him the smocked gown.

Hope was beautifully clothed in death. But, oh, how much more beautifully clothed she will be in the resurrection! She and all who are in Christ will be clothed in pure holiness, astounding beauty, and radiant glory. Right now, only Jesus is fully clothed with this resurrection glory. But he is just the first.

My friends, our future is not a return to the nakedness of the garden of Eden. Instead, Christ has made it possible for all who are joined to him to be clothed with immortality. We'll be holy through and through, so glorious we'll need new eyes to be able to look at each other. We're going to be so, so beautiful—beautiful like Jesus. When the man of heaven, the glorious risen Christ, returns to this earth, we're going to be wearing the same thing he's wearing. And we won't be embarrassed by it. We'll glory in it. And until then we sing:

> Nothing in my hand I bring,
> simply to Thy cross I cling;
> Naked, come to Thee for dress;
> helpless, look to Thee for grace;
> Foul, I to the fountain fly;
> Wash me, Savior, or I die.

> While I draw this fleeting breath,
> When my eyes shall close in death,
> When I rise to worlds unknown,
> And behold Thee on Thy throne,
> Rock of Ages, cleft for me,
> Let me hide myself in Thee.[13]

5

The Story of the Bridegroom

The passion of the world's greatest romances echoes down through history in the form of poetry. And my great romance is no exception. I'd like to say that this ode to our love was prompted simply by an overflow of affection bubbling from my husband's heart, but as I remember, it was actually a last-minute composition before a young married Valentine's Day party in the early nineties in which husbands were instructed to write and read a poem to their wives at the gathering. Never wanting to be outdone in the clever-rhyme department, David wowed the crowd with this:

> If I were a termite
> And you were a chair,
> I'd nibble your leg
> 'til nothing was there.

> If you were September
> And I were July,
> I'd trade places with August
> To be by your side.
>
> But I'm not a termite
> No, I'm just a man,
> And so I will love you
> The best that I can.
>
> And yet, may I ask you
> In fact, even beg —
> Would you still allow me
> To nibble your leg?[1]

A while later, though far less skilled in the art of poetic expression of affection, I responded to David's heartfelt soliloquy:

> If I were a flower
> and you were a bee,
> I'd open my petals
> so you'd buzz around me.
>
> If you were March
> and I was May,
> I'd trade places with April
> if for only one day.
>
> But you are a man
> And I am your wife.
> I look forward to loving you
> all of my life.
>
> But could I just ask you,
> if you were a bee,
> when looking for flowers
> would you still pick me?

Love loves to be expressed in poetic verse. Think of this opening line from Elizabeth Barrett Browning's Sonnets from the Portuguese 43:

How do I love thee? Let me count the ways.
I love thee to the depth and breadth and height
My soul can reach . . .

And its closing line:

I love thee with the breath,
Smiles, tears, of all my life; and, if God choose,
I shall but love thee better after death.

There is something so glorious about love between a man and a woman, something so intoxicating, so breathtaking, that ordinary sentences just won't do to express it. So it makes sense that in the love story that is the Bible, the first recorded human words are love poetry. In Genesis 2 we find an outburst of breathless joy from the heart of Adam as he falls in love with Eve, the original bride. He exclaims:

This at last is bone of my bones
    and flesh of my flesh. (Gen. 2:23)

It makes sense that the Bible would begin with this poetic exclamation of love because the Bible is a love story from beginning to end. It's the story of God choosing, gathering, and beautifying a bride for his Son. She's not necessarily the prettiest or the most loving in return. In fact, as we read the story of the bride, we're a little shocked at times that God would chose her. We see that she often has a hard heart; she's often resistant to his affections and wholly dismissive of his gifts. Yet the Father is relentless in his pursuit and preparation of this bride for his Son. So far, it's proving to be an unexpectedly long engagement. The Father has set a date for the wedding, and the invitations have been sent out. Of course, as much as we anticipate that day, the wedding will be only the beginning. It is the eternal marriage, the one in which we'll never have to say, "Till death do us part," that we anticipate most—a marriage that will be even better than the marriage Adam and Eve enjoyed in Eden.

The Original Bride

It seems that there's a lot of over-the-top pressure these days when it comes to weddings. The poor guy not only has to work up the courage to ask the girl; he has to make a production of the proposal, complete with photographer and perhaps videographer. And then there's the creation of a wedding website that includes an "our story" section about how the couple met and got engaged. I suppose if there had been such a thing as wedding websites in the days of Eden, that section on Adam and Eve's wedding website would have read, "The LORD God took the man and put him in the garden of Eden to work it and keep it. . . . Then the LORD God said, 'It is not good that the man should be alone; I will make him a helper fit for him'" (Gen. 2:15, 18).

Adam, the only human in Eden, had this enormous task out in front of him of filling, subduing, and ruling over the earth under God's authority. And as God looked at the situation, he deemed that it was "not good" for Adam to be alone. The text doesn't say that Adam was lonely. To assume that God was about to give Adam a wife merely to address a sense of loneliness would be to read something into it. If companionship was the issue, then it seems as though the verse would say that God made a companion for him. In actuality, the issue seems to be that the job that Adam had been given was too big for him to do on his own.[2] So Adam was given a helper. "The woman would make it possible for man to do what he could never do alone."[3] The account in Genesis seems to push back on all our overly romantic notions of marriage, as it reveals to us that the purpose of marriage, then and now, is not most profoundly about companionship or sexual fulfillment. Though it certainly has the potential to provide those wonderful things, the original, and still primary, purpose or aim of marriage in God's world is to serve the purposes of God in the world.[4]

Now maybe that word used to describe Eve—*helper*—rubs you the wrong way. Perhaps it hits you as somehow diminishing of her or of women in general. It's important to note that God himself is described as a helper throughout the Bible, especially in terms of doing battle against Israel's enemies.[5] So to help with the task of filling, subduing, and ruling over the earth is a very Godlike, noble thing.

Moses describes the creation of the woman and her introduction to the man:

> So the LORD God caused a deep sleep to fall upon the man, and while he slept took one of his ribs and closed up its place with flesh. And the rib that the LORD God had taken from the man he made into a woman and brought her to the man. (Gen. 2:21–22)

A divinely arranged marriage. No eHarmony required. There in the lush garden, by the river that flowed out of Eden, God brought a bride to his son, Adam, and presented her to him. Adam took one of the world's best naps, woke up to one of God's greatest gifts, and took part in the world's first wedding. Like the father of a bride, the Lord God led Eve to Adam, and Adam's response to his bride became the world's first recorded human words, a love poem:

> Then the man said,
>
> > "This at last is bone of my bones
> >   and flesh of my flesh;
> > she shall be called Woman,
> >   because she was taken out of Man." (Gen. 2:23)

An outburst of joy from the heart of Adam. "At last!" he exclaimed. All the animals had been paraded past Adam so that he could name them. And while they lived and breathed like he did, none of them could be his partner in this great task God had given to him. "At last!" expresses the requited longing of Adam for another creature who was like him—not a duplicate, but rather a fitting complement. God fashioned Eve from Adam's own flesh but, like a true artist, refined his original work, giving her softer curves and more refined features.

Following this poetic exclamation from Adam, it's as if the narrator of this love story turns and speaks directly to his original readers, and also to us, helping us make the connection between this first marriage in Eden to every other marriage since then: "Therefore a man shall leave his father and his mother and hold fast to his wife, and they shall become one flesh" (Gen. 2:24).

Marriage is meant to be a lifelong, one-flesh union of complete self-surrender, even more profound than the parent-child relationship. To be married is to share everything—bodies, money, hopes, troubles, successes and failures, sickness and health, until separated by death. Ray Ortlund puts it: "Two selfish me's start learning to think like one unified us."[6] In this first marriage, Adam and Eve had nothing to hide, nothing to protect, and everything to share. Their present was rich in relationship, and their future was bright with purpose and possibility.

Wouldn't it be great if we could stop the story of human marriage right there? Wouldn't it be wonderful if we all had Eve's experience of being celebrated and cherished as a bride, of having marriages that were as intimate and untouched by boredom, disappointment, betrayal, alienation, frustration, failure, or death as Adam and Eve's marriage was at this point in the story?

Instead, as the story progresses, the way things were created to work in Genesis 2 is inverted in Genesis 3. Animals were supposed to be ruled by the man, but in Genesis 3 a creeping thing gets the upper hand. The woman was supposed to be a helper to the man in carrying out God's commands, but instead she became a hindrance. The man was supposed to exercise gracious leadership of his wife and protect her from harm, but instead he abdicated his responsibility, leaving her vulnerable to deception.

We can hardly believe that the same two people who were naked and unashamed are, only a few verses later, trying to cover up their shame. We can hardly believe that the same person who held out his hand to the woman to welcome her, exclaiming, "At last!" only a few verses later points the finger of blame in her direction, saying, "The woman whom you gave to be with me, she gave me fruit of the tree, and I ate" (Gen. 3:12).

This was a marriage with a mission—to fill the earth with off-spring, to subdue it, and to rule over it. This was a match made in heaven on the earth. Yet this marriage, like so many marriages, went terribly wrong. This partnership that was intended to bless the world brought a curse upon the world. Initial delight dissolved into order-rejecting, blame-shifting, guilt-driven hiding, alienation, and conflict. Genesis 3 explains why many people who get married with high hopes find themselves nursing broken hearts:

To the woman [God] said,

> "I will greatly multiply
> Your pain in childbirth,
> In pain you will bring forth children;
> Yet your desire will be for your husband,
> And he will rule over you." (Gen. 3:16 NASB)

God tells Adam and Eve that the curse will work its way into the one-flesh relationship they enjoy and the mission they are on, so that it will be altered forever in three specific ways. First, instead of painlessly filling the earth with offspring, fulfilling that part of their task will hurt. God wasn't just talking about the pain of childbirth. There is no epidural powerful enough to overcome the pain that is connected not only to birthing but also to being a sinner raising a sinful child in this sin-cursed world. Don't we sometimes wish there was some way to numb ourselves to the deep hurts that our deep love for our children, or our deep desire to have children, create in our lives? The deep hurt of seeing our child left out or fall behind, overwhelmed, or underestimated? Until we became parents, we simply didn't know how much we could ache over the pain a child feels or the lifestyle a child has pursued. But any parent, or anyone who has desperately wanted to be a parent, would never dispute, "In pain you shall bring forth children."

God told Eve that her "desire will be for [her] husband." We want to desire our husband, so this doesn't initially sound like a problem. And, honestly, the way we are to understand what *desire* means in this verse is disputed.[7] But it does seem helpful that the same word is used in the very next chapter, and that both times it is God speaking, so we would anticipate a consistency in meaning. When we turn the page from Genesis 3 to Genesis 4, we see that Adam and Eve's son Cain was so jealous that he wanted to kill his brother Abel. The Lord said to Cain, "sin is crouching at the door. Its *desire* is contrary to you, but you must rule over it" (Gen. 4:7). Clearly sin wanted to master Cain; it wanted to tell Cain what to do, which was to kill his brother Abel. So this offers us some insight into what God was saying to the woman in the previous chapter. The sin that she committed had pervasively changed her and her husband and therefore changed their relationship. She was made to come alongside him to help in the mission God gave to them, but now his leadership in the mission would be a constant rub. Sin would warp the way he was intended to lead. Instead of lovingly and graciously leading the way in serving God together, he would tend toward harsh, overbearing, even exploitive leadership, or offer little or no leadership. Instead of ruling with her, he would seek to rule over her. In other words, their marriage would be desperately in need of grace, just like every marriage since then.

It must have been clear to Adam and Eve at this point, and it's certainly clear to us, that we're not in paradise anymore. Yet their love story did not end in total disaster but rather in hope. In the midst of the curse came a promise that filled them with hope for the future. The promise of a child who would one day be born as their descendant, who would crush the head of the Serpent, instilled in Adam and Eve a sense of anticipation. They began to anticipate the birth of a second Adam who would be a more faithful bridegroom than the first Adam, as well as a second Eve who would be a pure bride in the way Eve failed to be.[8]

And we find ourselves somewhere in the middle of this grand story. We know what it's like to experience the longing Adam experienced in Eden for someone to share life with—not our duplicate or our opposite, but our complement. And some of us know what it's like to find ourselves saying, "At last—at last I found him!" But some of us also know what it's like to lose the one we thought was "the one." Some of us know what it's like to be in a marriage that started out with promise and purpose but, because of sin—his, hers, ours— has become marked by disappointment, conflict, and perhaps even divorce. And some of us wonder if we will ever get to say, "At last!"— if our complement will ever come along.

So what does this marriage in Eden, in fact, marriage throughout the Scriptures and up to the present, have to say to those of us who dare to hope that the utter delight of boy meets girl, expressed in the world's first love poem, could be not only restored but also exceeded? Plenty. Every one of us is invited into the happily-ever-after of this story.

The Beloved Bride

Ever since the first marriage went so terribly wrong, God has been working out his plan to present a perfected bride to the perfect groom. You could call the history of the world the world's longest engagement. But nothing can prevent these nuptials from taking place. And the marriage is sure to be worth all the waiting. God began by calling one less-than-perfect couple to himself, Abraham and Sarah, and blessing their marriage with a son named Isaac. When it came time for Isaac to have a wife, Abraham didn't want him to marry a daughter of the Canaanites, so he sent his trusted servant back to the country he came from to find a wife for his son from among his relatives. His servant traveled to the city of Nahor and waited by the well outside the city for the time of day when women went out to draw water. (I guess if you don't have matchmaking websites, waiting by the well is the best way to survey possible marriage candidates.) Isaac was the son of the promise, and God was going to bring a bride for him to this well. Sure enough, Rebekah came out to the well. She was the one. God brought a bride for Abraham's son to the well so that wedding plans could begin.

Isaac and Rebekah went on to have two sons, Esau and Jacob, and the day came when Jacob traveled to this same land. He was standing by a well when Rachel approached with her father's flocks. Genesis 29 tells us:

> Now as soon as Jacob saw Rachel the daughter of Laban his mother's brother, and the sheep of Laban his mother's brother, Jacob came near and rolled the stone from the well's mouth and watered the flock of Laban his mother's brother. Then Jacob kissed Rachel and wept aloud. (Gen. 29:10–11)

Evidently it was love at first sight. He was smitten. There's a sense of "At last!" Again, God brought a bride, this time for Jacob, to a well.

Four hundred years later we see that Jacob's twelve sons had been fruitful and multiplied and had become a people two million strong. But they were living as slaves in Egypt. Moses had wanted to deliver them, but his plan went all wrong. So he fled from Egypt and went to the land of Midian and sat down by a well. Seven daughters of the priest of Midian came to the well to draw water for their father's flock, but one of them, Zipporah, found a husband there that day. God brought a bride for Moses to the well.

But these were not the only brides in the Old Testament. It was Israel, the people of God, who was featured on the cover of bridal magazines throughout the Old Testament. Throughout the Old Testament we see God at work among his people, preparing them to be a bride. That's how he saw Israel—as his bride: "For your Maker is your husband, / the LORD of hosts is his name," writes the prophet Isaiah (Isa. 54:5). God brought his bride Israel out to the wilderness. There in the wilderness she became so very thirsty—both physically and spiritually. So God opened up a well for her in the middle of a desert, providing water from a rock to quench her thirst. He gave her a home and came down to live with her in that home. He loved her and led her and took care of her. But the history of Israel was made up of one adulterous affair after another. God's beloved bride was always running off to the high places to have sexual liaisons in the worship of other gods.

The Ruined Bride

Sadly, the marriage between God and his bride, Israel, which started out with such promise, went very wrong. We get to hear the Lord, through the prophet Jeremiah, wistfully remembering how his love story with Israel began:

Thus says the LORD,

"I remember the devotion of your youth,
    your love as a bride,

> how you followed me in the wilderness,
> in a land not sown." (Jer. 2:2)

Before they entered the land, God had made clear that what he wanted was their heart: "You shall love the LORD your God with all your heart and with all your soul and with all your might. . . . You shall not go after other gods, the gods of the peoples who are around you—for the LORD your God in your midst is a jealous God" (Deut. 6:5, 14–15). He also made clear that Israel was the object of his affection:

> It was not because you were more in number than any other people that the LORD set his love on you and chose you, for you were the fewest of all peoples, but it is because the LORD loves you and is keeping the oath that he swore to your fathers, that the LORD has brought you out with a mighty hand and redeemed you from the house of slavery, from the hand of Pharaoh king of Egypt. (Deut. 7:7–8)

God gave his bride a book of love poetry that should have helped her see how very beautiful and fulfilling he intended their love relationship to be—the Song of Solomon. In this book of wisdom, God painted a picture of a passionate romance in the form of poetry between a bridegroom and a bride who are breathlessly and hopelessly in love. He spoke of a love that is "strong as death. . . . Its flashes are flashes of fire, the very flame of the LORD" (Song 8:6). This song should have fanned the flames of longing for the Bridegroom in the hearts of God's people. It should have filled Israel with confident expectation of an all-satisfying romance that would keep her watching and waiting for her Bridegroom. But she was stubborn in her adulterous ways.

So God sent a prophet named Hosea. Hosea was called not simply to confront God's adulterous wife with words; rather, his own marriage to an unfaithful bride would provide Israel with a vivid picture of her repeated and ruinous unfaithfulness:

> When the LORD first spoke through Hosea, the LORD said to Hosea, "Go, take to yourself a wife of whoredom and have children of

whoredom, for the land commits great whoredom by forsaking the LORD." (Hos. 1:2)

But Hosea set in front of them more than just a picture of a bad marriage. Hosea's relentless love for an unfaithful bride also set before Israel a picture of what God intended to do as the Bridegroom. After Gomer had been used up by her lovers and was being auctioned off to whoever might buy her, Hosea heard the Lord tell him, "Go again, love a woman who is loved by another man and is an adulteress, even as the LORD loves the children of Israel, though they turn to other gods." And Hosea recounts, "So I bought her for fifteen shekels of silver and a homer and a lethech of barley. And I said to her, 'You must dwell as mine for many days. You shall not play the whore, or belong to another man; so will I also be to you'" (Hos. 3:1–3). In his relentless, redeeming love for an unworthy, adulterous bride, Hosea set before the people of God in his day a preview of the relentless, redeeming, sanctifying love of our divine Bridegroom.

Clearly God had not given up on his quest to present his Son with a bride. To give Israel hope of his coming, he gave the prophet Isaiah a vision of a future wedding day:

> You shall no more be termed Forsaken,
>   and your land shall no more be termed Desolate,
> but you shall be called My Delight Is in Her,
>   and your land Married;
> for the LORD delights in you,
>   and your land shall be married.
> For as a young man marries a young woman,
>   so shall your sons marry you,
> and as the bridegroom rejoices over the bride,
>   so shall your God rejoice over you. (Isa. 62:4–5)

The prophet was looking into the future, and he saw Desolate getting married and living happily ever after. It's a moving picture. But, honestly, does it not strain credulity to think that this ruined bride could ever become pure enough, or beautiful enough, to be acceptable to her holy Bridegroom? The hopelessness of the situation caused many to stop looking for this holy husband. Instead, they settled into a passionless relationship with God, simply going through the motions. They honored God with their lips, but their hearts were far from him (Mark 7:6).

The Bridegroom

Finally, after four hundred years with no word on the wedding, John the Baptist appeared on the scene, calling himself "the friend of the bridegroom" (John 3:29). At just the right time, the Bridegroom came. We find him at the very beginning of his ministry at a wedding in Cana, at which there was a big problem. During this era, the bridegroom was responsible for supplying wine for the celebration, but at this particular wedding, they'd run out of wine. Fortunately, the true and faithful Bridegroom was there, doing what a bridegroom was supposed to do. But this Bridegroom was superior to every other bridegroom. Jesus provided such exquisite water-become-wine, the wedding guests thought that the other groom had simply saved the best for last. It's as if the Gospel writer wanted us to see right off who Jesus really is—the true Bridegroom, the one God's people had been waiting for ever since the first bridegroom, Adam, failed so miserably in Eden.

Soon after this wedding in Cana, John the Baptist's disciples come to him with concerns that people were going to Jesus's disciples to be baptized instead of coming to John. But John responded, "The one who has the bride is the bridegroom. The friend of the bridegroom, who stands and hears him, rejoices greatly at the bridegroom's voice" (John 3:29). John the Baptist, as the final Old Testament prophet, knew that it was the voice of this Bridegroom that God's people had most longed to hear. If only they would recognize his voice. If only they would come as he opened his arms and his heart to them.

But the reality is that "he came to his own, and his own people did not receive him" (John 1:11). Perhaps part of the problem was that this Bridegroom was interested in having a bride far more exotic and diverse than the Jews had anticipated. This bride was meant to be made up of people from every nation. In chapter 4 of John's

Gospel, we witness Jesus pass through Samaria (a faux pas for any self-respecting Jew) and head straight for Jacob's well. There, Jesus encountered the most unlikely prospect to bind to himself in marriage.

She went to the well at an unusual time of day because she simply couldn't face all the other women in town since she'd probably slept with some of their husbands. Her history was a litany of failed marriages, and at that point she was sleeping with a man she was not married to. None of her previous grooms had proved faithful. They'd just used her, and she'd used them, and her life had become a shame-filled, brokenhearted mess. But then she arrived at the well, and she met a man who knew all about her past and still offered himself to her, saying, "Everyone who drinks of this water will be thirsty again, but whoever drinks of the water that I will give him will never be thirsty again. The water that I will give him will become in him a spring of water welling up to eternal life" (John 4:13–14).

Once again, God had brought a bride to the well. She was from the other side of the tracks with a shameful sexual history. And she was thirsty, so very, very thirsty. She had an unquenchable thirst to be loved, to be satisfied beyond a moment of pleasure, to be accepted and nurtured and cherished. At first she thought Jesus was a prophet. But eventually she and many other Samaritans in her town recognized that he was the Savior of the world, the second Adam, the true and faithful Bridegroom, and that he was inviting them—those who hadn't come from the right family, those with checkered pasts, those who would never presume to wear white when walking down the aisle—to become joined to him in a marriage that will last forever.

Perhaps this eternal marriage is what Jesus was getting at when the Sadducees came to him with a question regarding a woman who'd been married to seven men over the course of a lifetime: which one would be her husband in the resurrection? Jesus's response was that they didn't understand the Scriptures or the power of God, because "in the resurrection they neither marry nor are given in marriage, but are like angels in heaven" (Matt. 22:30).

For some of us, the idea that we will not be married to the person we have loved dearly in this life sounds as if it just can't be right.

But evidently marriage as we know it is uniquely for this age. That doesn't, however, mean that there won't be rich relationship in the age to come. In fact, our relationships with those we have loved will be deepened, as sin will no longer infect or inhibit our connections to one another. John Piper writes, "There will be no marriage there. But what marriage meant will be there. And the pleasure of marriage, ten-to-the-millionth power, will be there."[9] Heaven will be rich in relationship—with each other and with the One we love the most—our glorious Bridegroom. In one sense, we'll all be married—and to the same Groom! The shadow of temporary human marriage will have given way to the substance—the eternal marriage between Christ and his bride. And this will be the happiest marriage of all time.

We will love him because he first loved us. In fact, no groom has ever loved or will ever love his bride the way that Christ has loved his:

> Christ loved the church and gave himself up for her, that he might sanctify her, having cleansed her by the washing of water with the word, so that he might present the church to himself in splendor, without spot or wrinkle or any such thing, that she might be holy and without blemish. (Eph. 5:25–27)

Oh, my friends, we have been, are now, and will forever be so well loved by our Bridegroom! Like the love of the bridegroom in Song of Solomon, the love of our Bridegroom was "as strong as death," even death on a cross. Like the bridegroom Hosea, our Bridegroom paid the cost to redeem his bride from slavery to sin and is even now sanctifying us to himself. One day this sanctification process will be complete. He who began a good work in us will be faithful to complete it at the day of Christ Jesus (Phil. 1:6). We are going to be the most beautiful bride who ever looked into the eyes of her groom.

The Beautiful Bride

God is bringing a bride to his Son, the second Adam, and presenting her to him. One day we are going to wake up from one of the best naps ever, to be a part of the greatest gift ever, to feast at the richest banquet ever, to gaze at the loveliest groom ever, to enjoy the best marriage ever—a marriage that will last forever. God is going to present us as a bride to our Bridegroom. The apostle John was given a preview of our wedding day:

> Then I saw a new heaven and a new earth, for the first heaven and the first earth had passed away, and the sea was no more. And I saw the holy city, new Jerusalem, coming down out of heaven from God, prepared as a bride adorned for her husband. (Rev. 21:1–2)

I imagine the Bridegroom on that day, his eyes fixed on his bride, unable to keep from bursting out with the same words the first Adam spoke when he first saw his bride: "At last!" At last we'll be all we were intended to be. At last the curse that brought such pain and conflict into our earthly marriages will be gone for good. At last we'll be together forever. "Behold, the dwelling place of God is with man. He will dwell with them, and they will be his people, and God himself will be with them as their God" (Rev. 21:3). No more separation, no more alienation.

This marriage is going to be so much better than the marriage of Adam and Eve in Eden. Our groom, the second Adam, will not fail to lovingly lead us to feast on the tree of life. He will not fail to protect us from evil. He will not dominate or abuse or ignore. He will not abandon. He will not die. His love will satisfy us forever in a home even better than Eden.

No human marriage, no matter how good, can bear the weight of our expectations of complete satisfaction and perfect harmony and intimacy that only this ultimate and eternal marriage can provide. After two sinners say, "I do," there is always at least a little, "What have I done?" But our less-than-perfect marriages or our longings to be married can serve to whet our appetite for this perfect marriage to come. Whether we're married or single, divorced or widowed, our lives are meant to be spent nurturing our longing for this better marriage. And someday that longing will be fulfilled. Don't stuff down those desires to be loved in this way; *direct your desires* toward the only one who can love you this way forever.

Don't think that because the Bridegroom has delayed his coming that he's not coming at all. Don't be like the five foolish bridesmaids who were unprepared. Jesus's parable of the bridegroom and the bridesmaids ended in what, for some of us, may seem an uncomfortable or even offensive way:

> The bridegroom came, and those who were ready went in with him to the marriage feast, and the door was shut. Afterward the other virgins came also, saying, "Lord, lord, open to us." But he answered, "Truly, I say to you, I do not know you." (Matt. 25:10–12)

Maybe that seems cold. Maybe when you read that, you think, *a God of love will never do that*. But it is precisely because he is a God of love and will do that that he sent Jesus to warn us.

It's precisely because he is a God of love that he has given his Word to us, which ends with an open invitation to all to come to the most expensive and extravagant wedding of all time. In the final chapter of the Bible we read, "The Spirit and the Bride say, 'Come.' And let the one who hears say, 'Come.' And let the one who is thirsty come; let the one who desires take the water of life without price" (Rev. 22:17). The Spirit and the bride are inviting all to come to this well of living water, Christ himself. Even now God is at work at this well, wooing and preparing a beautiful bride for his beloved Son. The Holy Spirit, speaking through the Word of God, is saying to you, "Come." All of those who are already being made ready for the wedding are saying, "Come." Say yes to this dress. Say yes to this Bridegroom.

In almost the last line of the last book of the Bible we get to hear our Bridegroom whisper words of hope into our ears: "He who testifies to these things says, 'Surely I am coming soon'" (Rev. 22:20). And we say in response: "Come quickly, Lord Jesus!"

On that day when he comes, I imagine our grand romance will still be best expressed in poetic verse. Perhaps we'll borrow from the Song of Solomon, the greatest love song of all time, as we look into the face of our glorious groom and say with radiant joy and a sense of relief, "'I am my beloved's and my beloved is mine.' Let's dance!" (see Song 6:3).

The church's one Foundation
is Jesus Christ her Lord;
she is His new creation,
by water and the Word;
from heav'n He came and sought her
to be His holy bride;
with His own blood He bought her,
and for her life He died.[10]

6

The Story of Sabbath

I don't recall what we were talking about in Sunday school one morning that led us into true confessions regarding gifting, or in my case, regifting. But for some unknown reason I told them (and I'm about to tell the world!) about my most embarrassing experience of regifting. I suppose that when couples get married, there's always one or two popular new kitchen gadgets or trendy items that they are given more than one of. Evidently the trendy item when I got married was the pump pot (a big thermos with a pump similar to those that hold coffee at Panera Bread). David and I got three of them. And I don't even drink coffee. So, when a college roommate got married a few months later, I picked out the nicest one I'd received and sent it to her as a gift. All was well until I received her thank-you note that said, "I'm enclosing the gift card written out to you that was inside the pot."

I'm still embarrassed.

But that Sunday morning my friend Bari had a story to top mine. After her first child was born, she unwrapped a gift from a friend and found a box of perfumed powder, or so she thought. Of course she knew better than to put that powder on her newborn, who needed to smell like Johnson and Johnson, so she put the unopened box of powder on the shelf intending to use it on herself at some point. She wrote a thank-you note to the friend who had given her the gift, extolling the virtues of the powder, telling her how lovely the powder smelled on the baby, etc. When her friend got the note, she called and suggested that Bari open the box. And when she did, there was no powder inside. Her friend had used the powder box to wrap a beautiful white satin music box. On first inspection, Bari had determined that the gift was something her baby didn't need, but when she opened the box, and appropriated the gift, it ended up bringing great delight to her and her children.

In this chapter we're going to talk about a gift—a gift about which we might initially think: *This is not for me. This is not something I want. This is not going to add to my life.* But when we open and appropriate this gift, we find that it fills our lives with a deep sense of meaning, gives us perspective, infuses us with hope, and generates real joy. Who wouldn't want that? God has a gift he wants to give that could fill up that fearful place with a solid sense of trust in his provision. This gift is meant to serve as a weekly course correction so that we will be able to see more clearly where we're headed and what is waiting there for us. Opening and appropriating this gift has the power to bring a restful rhythm to our lives.

God has given us the gift of a day—one day different from all the other days in our week—to push away from the table of the world that fills us up with its amusements and technology and weighs us down with its expectations and commitments. This gift invites us, instead, to pull up a chair at the table where God himself wants to fill us up with himself and to take on himself all the things that are weighing on us.

But let's be honest. Many of us get a little bit nervous when the topic of Sabbath or the Lord's Day comes up, because we're afraid that we are using God's day in a way that we shouldn't, and, really, we'd rather keep on doing that thing. In other words, we don't see what God has set before us—keeping one day in seven as holy to him—as a gift but rather as a restriction. We think anything we do to restrict how we use this day is going to take away from our life, that it will become less pleasurable, less satisfying, less stimulating, and, honestly, far less interesting than what we like to do. We've come to see it as *our* day, not *his* day. We're happy to give him about ninety minutes of this day, or maybe even three hours if we're going to Sunday school as well as worship, or to small group as well as the service, but we often find ourselves watching the clock because we want to get on with what we really want to do—get to the game, take a nap, work on a project, tune in to a show, get ready for the coming week. There is a voice inside some of us that says, "This is *my* time to do with as I please." Yet he who created time intends that time itself bear witness to *his* purposes in the world and in his people.

Some of us have come to see any kind of restriction on what we do or don't do with this day as old-fashioned legalism, and we certainly don't want any of that. So we don't set any restrictions. We don't make any preparations. And while we're not out to do anything evil or unseemly with this day, the truth is, our day looks pretty much like our unbelieving neighbor's day except, perhaps, for the hour or two we spend at church.

So if that's ever going to change, or if we're going to become convinced that it even needs to change, we're going to have to understand why God established one day in seven to be set aside for him in the first place. Perhaps if we get a better grasp on why he wanted to give us this day as a gift, we'll be willing to loosen our grip on using it our way. Until then, any suggestion of setting aside a day as holy will seem like legalism or mere traditionalism.

The Promise of Rest in Eden

When we read about the creation of the world in Genesis 1, a pattern develops. Six times we read, "There was evening and there was morning, the _____ day." But when we get to the seventh day, something is missing. We read:

> On the seventh day God finished his work that he had done,
> and he rested on the seventh day from all his work that he had
> done. So God blessed the seventh day and made it holy, because
> on it God rested from all his work that he had done in creation.
> (Gen. 2:2–3)

There's no "evening and morning, the seventh day." Chad Bird writes,
"It's as if this day never ended, that it is waiting for something—
or someone—to bring it to a close."[1]

God had done his work of creation, and then he rested. The Father
had finished his work, but Adam had not. Adam was given work to
do in Eden. He was to (1) fill the earth with image-bearing offspring,
(2) subdue the earth by extending the cultivated garden beyond the
boundaries of Eden, and (3) exercise dominion over the creation by
guarding it from evil. But this task was not limitless. There was an end
or goal. Had Adam applied himself to the work, the day of completion would have come.[2] He, like God, would have been able to say,
"It is finished. I have completed the work you have given me to do."
And God would have said to Adam and Eve and all of their posterity,
"Well done, good and faithful servant. You have been faithful over
a little; I will set you over much. Enter into the joy of your master"
(Matt. 25:21).

In resting from his work of creation when it was done, God was
setting before Adam something to look forward to when Adam's work
of subduing the earth, exercising dominion over it, and filling it with
image bearers was done.[3] There was an implied promise: "Work, and
you will rest with me." To keep Adam oriented toward this goal, and
from losing sight of this promised rest, Adam was to emulate the divine pattern of working six days and resting on the seventh day.[4] We
don't know how long this pattern of work and rest would have continued until Adam had completed his work and entered into a permanent Sabbath rest.[5] But what we do see is that Eden at the beginning
was not like it was intended to be forever. Even in Eden, history was
headed somewhere. It was headed toward an unending, all-satisfying
rest in the presence of God. If Adam had obeyed and completed the
work, he would have brought all of humanity into this rest. But, of

course, Adam failed in the work he was given to do. He didn't exercise dominion over the evil Serpent or his own appetites. So instead of leading us into rest, Adam plunged us into the restlessness inherent in a sin-corrupted world.

There was only one way for the people of God to enter into the eternal rest God had planned for his people. It would require another Adam, another representative of God's people, to complete the work.[6] When Adam and Eve's son Cain was born, Eve celebrated, saying, "I have gotten a man with the help of the LORD" (Gen. 4:1). She must have hoped that this son was the promised descendant who would lead them into rest. But he was so restless, so unable to rule over even himself, let alone the creation, that he killed his brother Abel. No rest yet. A few generations later, when Lamech fathered a son, he "called his name Noah, saying, 'Out of the ground that the LORD has cursed, this one shall bring us relief from our work and from the painful toil of our hands'" (Gen. 5:29). Perhaps Noah was the one who would bring God's people into rest.

When Noah came out of the ark into the new creation, God assigned to him the same work that Adam had been given to do in the first creation:

> God blessed Noah and his sons and said to them, "Be fruitful and multiply and fill the earth. The fear of you and the dread of you shall be upon every beast of the earth and upon every bird of the heavens, upon everything that creeps on the ground and all the fish of the sea. Into your hand they are delivered. (Gen. 9:1–2)

Fruitfulness and multiplication, subduing, and dominion. But only a few verses after these verses that detail the work assigned to Noah, we find the record of his failure to do it. The problem here wasn't eating the fruit of a tree, but drinking the fruit of a vine and becoming drunk. Another failure that led to shameful nakedness. Another failure to subdue and rule over creation. No rest yet.

A few generations later, when God appeared to Abraham, it was clear that the original purpose God had for Adam in Eden was still in play. But instead of issuing a command, God gave Abraham a promise.

Instead of commanding him to be fruitful, God promised to make him fruitful. His offspring would be as numerous as the sand on the seashore or stars in the sky. Instead of commanding him to exercise dominion over nature, God promised to give him possession of the land of Canaan and to subdue the enemies there.

The Reminder of Rest in the Wilderness

When we read in the first chapter of Exodus, "The people of Israel were fruitful and increased greatly" (v. 7), it is evident that God had indeed made Abraham's offspring fruitful. But they were certainly not at rest. They were slaves, likely working seven days a week for the Egyptian pharaoh. So when they came out of Egypt, crossed the Red Sea, and were immediately given the command to keep the Sabbath, it must have seemed like a great gift (Ex. 16:22–30). Later Moses brought down from Mount Sinai two stone tablets that told the people of God how they were to live once they were settled in the land God was giving to them. On those stone tablets was this command:

> Remember the Sabbath day, to keep it holy. Six days you shall labor, and do all your work, but the seventh day is a Sabbath to the LORD your God. On it you shall not do any work, you, or your son, or your daughter, your male servant, or your female servant, or your livestock, or the sojourner who is within your gates. For in six days the LORD made heaven and earth, the sea, and all that is in them, and rested on the seventh day. Therefore the LORD blessed the Sabbath day and made it holy. (Ex. 20:8–11)

The weekly Sabbath was intended to jog Israel's collective memory concerning God's sufficiency and supply in the past and his promise concerning the future. They were to remember his work of creation as well as his work of redemption. It was to serve as an ever-present sign of loving relationship between God and his people. Before Moses headed down the mountain with the tablets, God reiterated the command: "You are to speak to the people of Israel and say, 'Above all you shall keep my Sabbaths, for this is a sign between me and you throughout your generations, that you may know that I, the LORD, *sanctify* you'" (Ex.

31:13). Sabbath keeping would set God's people apart as being so well taken care of by their God that they could take a day to rest. It would set them apart as a people who had something to look forward to: unending, all-encompassing rest in the presence of the one true God.

It wasn't just the rhythm of their weeks that was to take this Sabbath shape. All their time, as well as their entire socioeconomic system, was to take this shape (see Leviticus 23; 25). Every seven years the land was to receive rest. There would be no plowing or sowing seed. God promised to provide enough harvest in the sixth year to last for three years so that they could give the land rest yet have a sufficient supply of food. In this way they would be reminded of the better land God was preparing and the provision God was making for their rest.

Every seven years was to be a sabbatical year. During this year, they were to release one another from debts incurred in the previous six years (Deut. 15:1). In this way they would be reminded of the freedom and forgiveness they would enjoy in their coming rest. Then every seven-times-seven years, there was to be a Year of Jubilee. At this time all lost or sold property would be returned to the tribe or clan to which Joshua had originally assigned it after they'd come into the Promised Land. In this way they would be regularly reminded that God would be faithful to preserve their inheritance, not merely in the Promised Land of Canaan, but in the ultimate promised land of the new heaven and the new earth, where they would experience ultimate and unending rest. God led his people into the Promised Land of Canaan with a promise that he would make them fruitful and that they would subdue the animal kingdom and exercise dominion:

> I will give peace in the land, and you shall lie down, and none shall make you afraid. And I will remove harmful beasts from the land, and the sword shall not go through your land. You shall chase your enemies, and they shall fall before you by the sword. Five of you shall chase a hundred, and a hundred of you shall chase ten thousand, and your enemies shall fall before you by the sword. I will turn to you and make you fruitful and multiply you and will confirm my covenant with you. (Lev. 26:6–9)

Perhaps Israel, as God's firstborn son, would collectively accomplish the work that Adam failed to accomplish. Perhaps Israel would dwell in this garden-like land, worshiping and serving God, multiplying the image of God and worship of him throughout the earth, and upon the completion of their work, enter the eternal Sabbath rest of God.[7] Perhaps the gift of rest given in the Sabbath would keep this sense of the meaning and purpose of their lives at the forefront of their minds and as the wellspring of their hearts.

Or perhaps not.

The Ruin of Rest in Canaan

Years later we hear the Lord say to his people through the prophet Ezekiel:

> I gave them my Sabbaths, as a sign between me and them, that they might know that I am the LORD who sanctifies them. But the house of Israel rebelled against me in the wilderness. They did not walk in my statutes but rejected my rules, by which, if a person does them, he shall live; and my Sabbaths they greatly profaned. (Ezek. 20:12–13)

The day God made holy, they made common, even dirty, because of the darkness of their hearts. Through the prophet Amos the Lord said:

> Hear this, you who trample on the needy
>   and bring the poor of the land to an end,
> saying, "When will the new moon be over,
>   that we may sell grain?
> And the Sabbath,
>   that we may offer wheat for sale,
> that we may make the ephah small and the shekel great
>   and deal deceitfully with false balances,
> that we may buy the poor for silver
>   and the needy for a pair of sandals
>   and sell the chaff of the wheat?"
>
> The LORD has sworn by the pride of Jacob:
> "Surely I will never forget any of their deeds.

Shall not the land tremble on this account,
>   and everyone mourn who dwells in it? (Amos 8:4–8)

God had given them the Sabbath, intending that his generous gift would make them generous to one another, but instead they used even the Sabbath to take advantage of one another. They didn't see the Sabbath as a gift. They saw it as a burden. Instead of allowing the Sabbath to shape their lives and their hopes, instead of using the day to nurture a love relationship with God, they pushed him away with their cruelty and hypocrisy. So much so that the prophet Isaiah spoke for God, saying:

> Bring no more vain offerings;
>   incense is an abomination to me.
> New moon and Sabbath and the calling of convocations—
>   I cannot endure iniquity and solemn assembly.
> Your new moons and your appointed feasts
>   my soul hates;
> they have become a burden to me;
>   I am weary of bearing them. (Isa. 1:13–14)

God had given them a gift, and what they did with the gift was an offense, a burden, to him. There's no record that God's people ever gave the land rest every seven years as they were instructed to do, so God gave the land rest. How? The Chronicler says:

> He took into exile in Babylon those who had escaped from the sword, and they became servants to him and to his sons until the establishment of the kingdom of Persia, to fulfill the word of the LORD by the mouth of Jeremiah, until the land had enjoyed its Sabbaths. All the days that it lay desolate it kept Sabbath, to fulfill seventy years. (2 Chron. 36:20–21)

After those seventy years, the day came when the people of God returned from exile in Babylon and under Nehemiah's leadership renewed their commitment to keep the Sabbath. They vowed: "If the peoples of the land bring in goods or any grain on the Sabbath day to sell, we will not buy from them on the Sabbath or on a holy day.

And we will forego the crops of the seventh year and the exaction of every debt" (Neh. 10:31). But just a short time later, Nehemiah returned to Jerusalem after a brief absence and made this exasperated observation:

> In those days I saw in Judah people treading winepresses on the Sabbath, and bringing in heaps of grain and loading them on donkeys, and also wine, grapes, figs, and all kinds of loads, which they brought into Jerusalem on the Sabbath day. And I warned them on the day when they sold food. Tyrians also, who lived in the city, brought in fish and all kinds of goods and sold them on the Sabbath to the people of Judah, in Jerusalem itself! (Neh. 13:15–16)

While Israel repeatedly failed to keep the Sabbath as God had commanded, the day came when her leaders sought to remedy the problem. They didn't do so with hearts turned toward God in joyful obedience; instead they heaped on additional rules. Legalism devoid of love for God robbed the Sabbath of its intended purpose and meaning, turning it into a burden instead of a gift. Clearly, if God's people were to have any hope of entering into the rest of God, there would have to be a second Adam, a true Israel, to accomplish the work Adam and Israel failed to accomplish and lead humanity into the rest they failed to reach.

The Revelation of Rest in Jesus

Jesus came into this world offering a personal invitation into the rest of God: "Come to me, all who labor and are heavy laden, and I will give you rest" (Matt. 11:28). Jesus made clear that the rest of God is not apprehended through our work but through his. Our work now is to put our faith and trust in his work. "This is the work of God," Jesus said, "that you believe in him whom he has sent" (John 6:29).

Jesus was fruitful and multiplied, calling to Simon and Andrew, "Follow me, and I will make you fishers of men." Jesus subdued the earth so that it obeyed his command. He told two weary fishermen to let down their nets, and they were filled with so many fish that their nets broke (Luke 5:5–6). He "rebuked the wind and said to the sea, 'Peace! Be still!' And the wind ceased, and there was a great calm" (Mark 4:39). Jesus exercised dominion over evil, refusing to let Satan misuse or distort God's word, repeatedly casting out demons from those under demonic oppression.

Whereas Adam hid from God in shame over his failure, Jesus was able to say to his Father, "I glorified you on earth, having accomplished the work that you gave me to do" (John 17:4). Of course the greatest work Christ accomplished happened as he hung on a Roman cross. It didn't look very fruitful; it didn't look like he was subduing the earth; it didn't look like he was exercising dominion. It looked like his efforts were pointless, like he was being subdued, like the offspring of the Serpent had won. This One who had promised rest experienced on the cross the greatest restlessness ever known to man, the restlessness that you and I deserve to endure forever. There on the cross he cried out, "My God, my God, why have you forsaken me?" (Matt. 27:46), which is also the first line of Psalm 22. It was as if Jesus was saying, "Psalm 22 is happening here." If he had continued to utter the words of the psalm, he would have said:

> *My God, my God, why have you forsaken me?*
>> Why are you so far from saving me, from the words of my
>>> groaning?
> O my God, I cry by day, but you do not answer,
>> and by night, but I find no rest. (Ps. 22:1–2)

It was the sixth day of the week when Christ cried out from the cross, "It is finished" (John 19:30). The work was done. On the cross Jesus accomplished his most fruitful work, the salvation of all who believe; he subdued the earth so that it shook in response. By canceling the record of debt that stood against us with its legal demands, nailing it to the cross, Jesus exercised dominion. "He disarmed the rulers and authorities and put them to open shame, by triumphing over them" (Col. 2:15). Jesus was put into the tomb, and then there was a day of rest, a Sabbath. "Having worked himself to death, Jesus rested from his labors."[8] Then came the first day of the week, the first day of the new creation, the day Jesus rose from the dead.[9]

Before ascending to the right hand of God, Jesus commissioned his disciples to continue the work of being fruitful and multiplying, of subduing the earth, of exercising dominion:

> All authority in heaven and on earth has been given to me. Go therefore and make disciples of all nations, baptizing them in the name of the Father and of the Son and of the Holy Spirit, teaching them to observe all that I have commanded you. And behold, I am with you always, to the end of the age. (Matt. 28:18–20)

Because this fruitfulness and multiplication come about through proclamation and embrace of the gospel instead of through giving birth, even those who have no physical children, like Paul, can boast of having many children.[10] Because of the work of the second Adam, Christ, carried out through his bride, the church, the new earth will one day be filled with his offspring, who have all been conformed to his likeness, a ransomed people for God from every tribe and language and people and nation (Rev. 5:9; 7:9).

The Rest That Remains

So where does this leave us in terms of keeping the Sabbath? Honestly, sound theologians have differing views.[11] Nowhere in the New Testament are we told explicitly to honor the Sabbath. In fact, there are some verses in the Epistles that might suggest otherwise (see Rom. 14:5; Gal. 4:10; Col. 2:16). We know that there were many aspects of the ceremonial law that once bound the people of God, laws that were actually a shadow of things to come—things that were fulfilled by Christ. Once the substance appeared—the person of Christ—there was no longer any need for the shadow. But we also see that there were some old-covenant shadows or signs that Jesus took and transformed into signs of the new covenant. On the night he was betrayed, Jesus took the feast of the Passover and infused it with new meaning as the Lord's Supper. Paul writes, "For whenever you eat this bread and drink this cup, you proclaim the Lord's death until he comes" (1 Cor. 11:26 NIV).

This supper is meant to keep our lives oriented around both the feast offered to us in Christ's atoning death and the future feast of the marriage supper of the Lamb. The sign of circumcision was replaced by the fuller sign of baptism (Col. 2:10–12), which not only causes us to look back at Christ's death and resurrection but also ahead to that day when his saving, sanctifying work in us will be complete, and we will rise from our graves in his perfect likeness. Likewise the Sabbath that was fulfilled in Christ was replaced with something. We see in the New Testament that believers in Christ began to gather on the first day of the week and to call it the Lord's Day (Acts 20:7; 1 Cor. 16:2; Rev. 1:10). While the old Sabbath pointed back to creation and redemption, the Lord's Day celebrates the new creation evidenced in the resurrection of Jesus.[12] We gather on the Lord's Day to remember creation and redemption as well as to anticipate the new creation. We are reminded that we are not yet at home with the Father; we're not yet walking with him in the new garden where we will see him face-to-face. We experience a measure of rest as we are joined to Christ in his death and resurrection, but we know there is a better, fuller, final rest in our future.

The writer of Hebrews wrote to first-century believers, "So then, there remains a Sabbath rest for the people of God, for whoever has entered God's rest has also rested from his works as God did from his. Let us therefore strive to enter that rest" (Heb. 4:9–11). He looks all the way back to Eden, when God rested after completing his work, and reiterates the promise that has been at the heart of observing the Sabbath throughout the centuries: the reality of a greater rest to which this day is just a pointer, a reminder, an opportunity for reorientation.

This is why a day of rest is still being held out to us as a gift. Since we haven't yet reached the sabbath rest that the weekly Sabbath pointed to, it makes sense that we would continue to set aside one day in seven to orient ourselves toward that future rest.[13] But the question we face is this: Are we willing to receive the gift this day is meant to be to us? If we've come to the unshakable conviction that God indeed commands us to set apart one day in seven to him, and if we truly fear God, we will sanctify his day. It simply won't be like every other day. We'll endeavor not to ruin it with either legalism or neglect. All the lists of do's and don'ts won't matter anymore because in our hearts we won't be wondering what we can get away with. Instead we'll joyfully apply ourselves to figuring out how we can get the most out of this gift.

My friends, the Lord's Day isn't given to us as a sports day. It isn't merely a family day. It's God's day. It's a day for works of necessity and works of mercy and works of piety that flow out of our desire to set apart the day for him.[14] If this day has been given to us as a gift, how do we start appropriating this gift in our lives? Maybe we start here: some of us have never read all the way through the Bible. Some of us haven't read one Christian book in the past year. Some of us would never commit to doing any outside preparatory work for a Bible study but would quickly say, "I don't have time." Really? God has given you a day for focusing on him, on all he has given to you and is preparing to give you. Couldn't you squeeze some time in there for listening to him by reading his Word? Some of us can't remember the last time we spent more than five minutes in thoughtful prayer. Wouldn't God's day be a great day to set aside time to talk to him? Some of us have never developed the habit of meditating on Scripture. Wouldn't God's day be a great day to think through, repeat, and perhaps even memorize a passage of Scripture so that it becomes a part of us? Wouldn't God's day be a great day to meet the need of someone we've been too busy to serve on the other six days?

Here's the thing: if the idea of pulling away from the television, the soccer sidelines, the office, or schoolwork so that we can focus our attention on God doesn't sound good to us, then the new creation will bore us.

This life was never meant to be an aimless existence; it has always been headed somewhere, somewhere better than Eden. The destination out in front of us should shape how we live day by day, week by week, and year by year. "Let us therefore strive to enter that rest." How? By resting in Christ's finished work and by spending a day, every week, anticipating the rest that is ahead for us because of it.

The day is coming when we will rise from sleep to an eternal day of rest that will never end. Wouldn't it be nice, in the restlessness of this world, to just spend a day, every week, in anticipation of that day?

Love divine, all loves excelling,
joy of heaven, to earth come down,
fix in us thy humble dwelling,
all thy faithful mercies crown.
Jesus, thou art all compassion,
pure, unbounded love thou art;
visit us with thy salvation;
enter every trembling heart.

Breathe, oh, breathe thy loving Spirit
into every troubled breast;
let us all in thee inherit;
let us find the promised rest.
Take away the love of sinning;
Alpha and Omega be;
end of faith, as its beginning,
set our hearts at liberty.

Come, Almighty, to deliver,
let us all thy life receive;
suddenly return, and never,
nevermore thy temples leave.
Thee we would be always blessing,
serve thee as thy hosts above,
pray and praise thee without ceasing,
glory in thy perfect love.

Finish, then, thy new creation;
pure and spotless let us be;
let us see thy great salvation
perfectly restored in thee:
changed from glory into glory,
till in heaven we take our place,
till we cast our crowns before thee,
lost in wonder, love and praise.[15]

7

The Story of Offspring

It was about six months after our daughter, Hope, died, and every-thing I read in the Bible seemed different. My Bible study assignment that week was to read Psalm 91 and to share with the group how it had been true in my life. Here's what I read:

> He who dwells in the shelter of the Most High
>   will abide in the shadow of the Almighty.
> I will say to the LORD, "My refuge and my fortress,
>   my God, in whom I trust."
>
> For he will deliver you from the snare of the fowler
>   and from the deadly pestilence.
> He will cover you with his pinions,
>   and under his wings you will find refuge;

his faithfulness is a shield and buckler.
You will not fear the terror of the night,
    nor the arrow that flies by day,
nor the pestilence that stalks in darkness,
    nor the destruction that wastes at noonday.

A thousand may fall at your side,
    ten thousand at your right hand,
    but it will not come near you.
You will only look with your eyes
    and see the recompense of the wicked.

Because you have made the LORD your dwelling place—
    the Most High, who is my refuge—
no evil shall be allowed to befall you,
    no plague come near your tent.

For he will command his angels concerning you
    to guard you in all your ways.
On their hands they will bear you up,
    lest you strike your foot against a stone.
You will tread on the lion and the adder;
    the young lion and the serpent you will trample
        underfoot.

Because he holds fast to me in love, I will deliver him;
    I will protect him, because he knows my name.
When he calls to me, I will answer him;
    I will be with him in trouble;
    I will rescue him and honor him.
With long life I will satisfy him
    and show him my salvation.

I remember sitting in that circle that day in tears. I had to say to the group, "I don't get how this is true. He *did* allow evil to befall us. A plague *did* come near our tent. In fact, he allowed something much worse to happen to us than striking a foot against a stone." It didn't seem that he had protected us at all.

The words on the page just didn't ring true or reliable. And yet I firmly believed that God's Word is true, that it is, in fact, the most solid and reliable truth in the universe. So I knew there had to be something wrong with the way I was reading and understanding this psalm. The message seemed to be that if you trust God, nothing bad will happen to you. Anyone who has walked with God for any length of time knows that isn't true, even though plenty of preachers try to sell that message based on passages like this. So what does this psalm really mean? And more significantly, what kind of protection can you and I really expect from God? Are we completely vulnerable to the evil forces in the world?

To get an answer, and insight on what this psalm and others like it are promising, we have to begin at the beginning, when evil first entered into the goodness of God's creation. We have to trace the story of the offspring of the Serpent and the offspring of the woman.

The Seduction of the Serpent

While Eden was created as good, it wasn't completely secure. There in the original garden, Adam and Eve were vulnerable to evil, deception, and even death. While we might not have thought of Eden this way before, it becomes obvious when we consider that evil inhabited the body of an ordinary serpent and brought death into the garden. It should have been a huge red flag for Eve when an animal started talking to her. She and Adam had been given authority over all the beasts of the field, and this beast of the field was talking back.

The Serpent's evil intentions were camouflaged as simply bringing an injustice, a falsehood on God's part, to the attention of Adam and Eve. "Did God actually say, 'You shall not eat of any tree in the garden'? . . . You will not surely die. For God knows that when you eat of it your eyes will be opened, and you will be like God, knowing good and evil" (Gen. 3:1, 4–5).

Adam should have detected the lie in the Serpent's twisting of God's word; he should have recognized the evil in the Serpent's suggestion; he should have crushed the head of this Serpent then and there. But instead he and Eve listened to the Serpent. By eating the fruit of the forbidden tree at his urging, they essentially transferred their allegiance to the Serpent.

It's a miracle—a divine mercy—that God didn't sweep down right then and there to put an end to the serpent and his new servants. Instead God came in grace, seeking out his erring children, covering them, and announcing a curse on this Serpent, which had caused so much harm.

So the LORD God said to the serpent, "Because you have done this,

> 'Cursed are you above all livestock
>> and all wild animals!
> You will crawl on your belly
>> and you will eat dust
>> all the days of your life.
> And I will put enmity
>> between you and the woman,
>> and between your offspring and hers;
> he will crush your head,
>> and you will strike his heel.'" (Gen. 3:14–15 NIV)

Though God ordained a world in which evil and rebellion were possible, he didn't create them. He is, however, clearly sovereign over them. Just as his word has the power to bless, so his word has the power to curse. He made clear that the days of this Evil One are numbered. One day a baby would be born, a descendant of the woman the Serpent had just deceived and so cruelly harmed. Her offspring would do the job Adam should have done. One day her offspring would crush the head of evil for good.

Occasionally when I walk on the trails at the wooded park near my house, I see a snake slithering across the path. It makes sense that you might find a snake in the woods. It's the stories of snakes found in other places that make my skin crawl. Just Google it. You'll find stories of snakes wrapped around car engines, a little snake found in a box of noodles, snakes coming out of vending machines, snakes under the sheets. I think we can all agree that nobody wants to find a snake under the sheets. But if you do come across a snake, what is the most obvious way to kill it? Stomp on its head. Cut off its head. Crush its head with a big rock. And if you're a snake (and, of course, you're not) what is the most likely way you'll try to take down a human as you slither across the ground, especially if said human is trying to crush your head? You'll strike at its heel.

Evidently that's a picture of what's going to happen in the climax of this epic battle God sets into motion in Eden. In the process of crushing the head of the Serpent, one particular offspring—notice that verse 15 has "he"—will experience the Serpent's poisonous fangs sinking into his heel. The poison of sin will deal a deathblow to this offspring.

But until this final battle, there will be plenty of skirmishes between the offspring of the woman and the offspring of the Serpent. If you are a peace lover at heart, someone who just wants everyone to be happy with everyone else, perhaps this announcement of an ongoing conflict sounds like miserable news. And in one sense it is, because we are constantly caught in this conflict. But in it is also good news. In sinning, Adam and Eve had sided with the Serpent and placed themselves in opposition to God. But in God's curse on the Serpent, God turned the tables. He put up a barrier of protection for them and their offspring that would inhibit them from making any kind of false peace with this evil Serpent. God made this failed king and queen his allies against the true Enemy. This ongoing enmity was for their benefit. God drove a wedge between the woman and the enemy of her soul, taking the initiative in her salvation.

It's the same initiative we need him to take in our lives. Apart from this work of divine grace and mercy we'll forever be at enmity with him instead of at enmity with the Evil One. In this curse on the Serpent it's as if God turns to Adam and Eve, who have rebelled against him and rejected his good gifts, and says, "I'm going to war, but not against you. I'm going to drive a wedge between you and this one who intends only harm against you. I am going to war on your behalf against your enemy."[1]

This war won't be limited, however, to Adam and Eve and this Serpent, or even to that one particular offspring and the Serpent. It will expand into on ongoing conflict between generations of the offspring of both the woman and the Serpent. Satan is the head of a kingdom of evil. While his offspring are not physical descendants, he has an army of evil spirits and unrepentant sinners who derive their nature from him.[2]

The Offspring of the Woman at War with the Offspring of the Serpent

This conflict erupted between Adam and Eve's very first offspring in the murderous rage of Cain toward his brother Abel. We're shown in this first generation that the "offspring of the woman" does not include every human being who will descend from Eve. The offspring of the woman are those whom God sets at enmity with Satan and makes peace with through Christ. While Eve was the mother of Cain as well as Abel in a physical sense, only Abel was her offspring in a spiritual sense. Though Cain was a physical descendant of Eve, he was a spiritual descendant of Satan.[3] From the very beginning of the Bible's story we see that family lineage is no guarantee of saving grace.

The book of Genesis, as well as other books in the Old Testament, takes great care to trace the line of the offspring. That's why there are all those genealogies in the Old Testament that you never want to be assigned to read in front of a group. Even though you might be tempted to skip or skim through them when they come up in your Bible reading, these genealogies are actually fascinating and important. They contain a tension that isn't obvious if we don't understand that we're tracing the story of the offspring. We're meant to be asking as we read: What will happen to the offspring of the woman? What will happen to the particular line through whom God intends the child to be born, the One who will put an end to this Enemy once and for all?

This ongoing battle and the threat to the offspring of the woman are at the heart of some of the most significant scenes in Old Testament history. When a famine threatens the lives of her offspring, Jacob's twelve sons flee to Egypt where there is grain. But four hundred years later they have been reduced to slaves in Egypt. The offspring of the woman is clearly at enmity with the offspring of the Serpent—the pharaoh, who had a serpent on his headdress, the symbol of where his power came from. The pharaoh was so determined to destroy the offspring of the woman that he told the midwives to kill every male child born to Hebrew women. And when that didn't work, he instructed that all the Hebrew male infants be thrown in the Nile River to drown. But one Hebrew boy floated his way to safety on the Nile right into the house of Pharaoh. He would be the one to deliver the offspring of the woman. The day would come when her offspring, two million strong, would stand and watch from the east side of the Red Sea while the offspring of the Serpent, the Egyptian army, was crushed by a wall of water.

As the offspring of the woman wandered in the wilderness for forty years, it was often hard to see any evidence that they were a family of faith. They complained about their leader and their food, accusing God of wanting to kill them in the desert. So God gave them a taste of their true Enemy. He sent fiery serpents to bite the people, and many died. God told Moses, "Make a fiery serpent and set it on a pole, and everyone who is bitten, when he sees it, shall live" (Num. 21:8). There on the pole was a bronze image of what was killing them—their sin, represented by a serpent. This was not a victorious serpent, but rather a defeated serpent, perhaps with its head crushed by the stake that pinned it to the pole.[4] All who put their faith in God's promise for deliverance and healing demonstrated that faith through their willingness to look at the bronze serpent on the pole, and they were saved from the poison of sin.

Years later, at home in the land that God promised, they once again found themselves in a fierce battle against the offspring of the Serpent—the Philistine army. But this time, one particular Philistine, Goliath of Gath, had a proposal. He proposed that Israel send out one soldier to do battle with him. If Israel's representative won, all the Philistines would become Israel's slaves; but if Goliath won, all Israel—the offspring of the woman—would become slaves to evil forever. Goliath came out covered in a coat of scale armor (1 Sam. 17:5). In other words, he was covered in a bronze breastplate that looked like the scales of a snake. And what did David, this offspring of the woman, do? With one small stone and a slingshot, he crushed the head of this offspring of the Serpent.

Centuries later the offspring of the woman was sent into exile, and one in particular, a young and beautiful woman named Esther, became the wife of Ahasuerus, the king of the Medes and the Persians. But an offspring of the Serpent was at work through Haman, who had a profound hatred for the Jews. He manipulated the king into signing a decree that on a particular day, everyone in the kingdom was to rise up "to destroy, to kill, and to annihilate all Jews" (Est. 3:13). We have to understand what this means from the perspective of the story the Bible is tracing. If all the Jews were killed, then no offspring of the woman would remain to one day crush the head of the Serpent's offspring. But Esther, the offspring of the woman, prevailed over Haman, the offspring of the Serpent, and he was put to death. We read that "the very day when the enemies of the Jews hoped to gain the mastery over them, the reverse occurred: the Jews gained mastery over those who hated them" (Est. 9:1). The offspring of the woman crushed the heads of the offspring of the Serpent.

The Coming of the Offspring of the Woman

Finally the day came when that one special offspring was born. "But when the fullness of time had come, God sent forth his Son, *born of woman*" (Gal. 4:4). Paul puts it that way so we'll see the connection between the birth of Jesus and the promise God made in Eden. This is the one, *the* offspring. No sooner was he born than it became clear that the battle was still raging. Matthew records, "Now after Jesus was born in Bethlehem of Judea in the days of Herod the king, behold, wise men from the east came to Jerusalem, saying, 'Where is he who has been born king of the Jews?'" (Matt. 2:1–2). Herod, the offspring of the Serpent, recognized the threat. But "an angel of the Lord appeared to Joseph in a dream and said, "Rise, take the child and his mother, and flee to Egypt, and remain there until I tell you, for Herod is about to search for the child, to destroy him" (Matt. 2:13).

The offspring of the Serpent lost that battle but did not give up. From the beginning of his ministry to its end, Jesus was constantly on the march against the powers of darkness. Almost immediately after he was tempted in the wilderness by Satan (who, by the way, quoted Psalm 91, twisting it to mean something it doesn't, like prosperity teachers do), Jesus faced an onslaught of opposition in Nazareth, a crowd so angry they wanted to throw him off a cliff (Luke 4:16–30). He went down to Capernaum and was in the synagogue on the Sabbath when a man with a demon "cried out with a loud voice, 'Ha! What have you to do with us, Jesus of Nazareth? Have you come to destroy us? I know who you are—the Holy One of God'" (Luke 4:33–34). The demons inhabiting this man, much as Satan had inhabited the serpent in Eden, recognized Jesus as the promised offspring Satan and his minions had been dreading all along, the offspring who had come to destroy them.

When we read the Gospels, we sometimes get the impression that demon possession was more common in that time and place than it is now. And there's a sense in which that's true. The reason we witness so much demonic activity in the Gospels is that the offspring of the woman had arrived on the scene to put an end to the work of the Devil, and all hell was let loose in an effort to thwart his crushing blow. The hosts of hell were shaking in their boots, fully aware of how this war will end.

All the minions of hell, whether or not they saw themselves that way, were also engaged in the conflict. The Jews in Jesus's day saw themselves on the side of all that is good, based on their blood relationship to Abraham. "Abraham is our father," they said to Jesus. But Jesus answered them, "If you were Abraham's children, you would be doing the works Abraham did, but now you seek to kill me, a man who has told you the truth that I heard from God. This is not what Abraham did. . . . You are of your father the devil, and your will is to do your father's desires" (John 8:39–44). They were physical offspring of Abraham but clearly spiritual offspring of the Devil.

The dividing line between the offspring of the Serpent and the offspring of the woman cuts through human families. That is why Jesus said:

> Do not think that I have come to bring peace to the earth. I have not come to bring peace, but a sword. For I have come to set a man against his father, and a daughter against her mother, and a

daughter-in-law against her mother-in-law. And a person's enemies will be those of his own household. (Matt. 10:34–36)

It's not that Jesus is a fan of family drama or conflict. It's that Jesus wants us to be clear that there is a family relationship that takes precedence over our blood relationships. What matters is whether we are joined by faith to his family or whether we are joined—by apathy toward, ignorance of, or outright rebellion against Christ—to the Father of Lies, the Accuser of the brethren, that ancient Serpent.

The Crushing of the Offspring of the Woman

As Judas chewed on a piece of bread he had just been fed by Jesus, we read that Satan entered into him. Satan thought this was going to be his finest hour. Indeed Jesus himself, as he was being seized by the soldiers at the behest of the religious leaders, said, "This is your hour, and the power of darkness" (Luke 22:53). After a series of trials that revealed the Enemy's true colors, the battle that had been raging ever since Eden came to a climax. This was the most intense battle, the most deadly as well as the most life-giving battle of all time, fought on the hill of Calvary.

Fifty days later Peter described what happened in the battle by saying that when Jesus was crucified and killed by the hands of lawless men, he was "delivered up according to the definite plan and foreknowledge of God" (Acts 2:23). And because we have been tracing the story of the offspring of the woman and the offspring of the Serpent, we know that is true. This bruising battle had been God's plan ever since Eden. That's what the prophet Isaiah was saying when he wrote:

> Yet it was the will of the LORD to crush him;
> > he has put him to grief;
> when his soul makes an offering for guilt,
> > he shall see his offspring; he shall prolong his days;
> the will of the LORD shall prosper in his hand. (Isa. 53:10)

Notice that Isaiah makes clear that this crushing of the woman's offspring will not ultimately end in defeat and death. "He shall prolong his days." He will emerge from being crushed for our iniquities to live forever. The will of the Lord—everything God intended to accomplish through the suffering of this Servant—will be accomplished. And don't miss this: "he shall see his offspring." The offspring of the woman will have offspring! His suffering will not be meaningless but rather prosperous, fruitful, and purposeful.

Here is the good news of the gospel found in the story of the offspring, a story that changes everything about how our story will end. "While we were enemies we were reconciled to God by the death of his Son" (Rom. 5:10). And, "We have peace with God through our Lord Jesus Christ" (Rom. 5:1). What good news of grace first delivered in the midst of the curse: enmity with Satan and peace with God made possible by the suffering of the woman's offspring.

In light of this promise of grace, true offspring of the woman put all their faith, all their hopes, and all their confidence for a future that is better than their past—better than they deserve—in the promised offspring. And we can be sure that the enemy of our souls wants to keep us from that.

And it is here that we begin to recognize that we are in the midst of a spiritual battle. "For we do not wrestle against flesh and blood, but against the rulers, against the authorities, against the cosmic powers over this present darkness, against the spiritual forces of evil in the heavenly places" (Eph. 6:12). The Enemy wants you to be in league with him, not at enmity with him. He wants to claim you as his own for eternity. And if you have children, he wants them too. So what do we do? We take up spiritual weapons to fight this spiritual battle. We saturate ourselves, and our homes, in the Word of God. Rather than presume upon God to save our children, we plead with God to save our children. We pray that our children will be at enmity with the Evil One and reconciled to God. We pray that they will not be deceived by the Devil's lies, nor linger in rebellion against God. We pray that they will recognize the voice of their Savior when he calls to them, that they will be clothed by him in the righteousness of Christ. We pray that they will take hold of the grace that was promised in the midst of the curse. We pray that when Christ sees his offspring, he will see the faces of our children.

The Crushing of the Offspring of the Serpent

The apostle John wrote: "The reason the Son of God appeared was to destroy the works of the devil" (1 John 3:8). John saw the death and resurrection of Jesus in light of the story of the offspring of the Serpent and the offspring of the woman. The list of our sins that Satan intended to use as a weapon against us was nailed to the cross so that in his death Jesus "disarmed the rulers and authorities and put them to open shame, by triumphing over them in him" (Col. 2:15). Jesus rose triumphantly from the grave that could not hold him and ascended to the right hand of the Father, where he remains until he comes again to destroy the ancient Serpent for good. Right now Satan is like a snake whose head has been crushed but whose tail is still whipping around and creating havoc. "Your adversary the devil prowls around like a roaring lion, seeking someone to devour" (1 Pet. 5:8). In a last-ditch effort to have his way in God's world, he is still at work against the offspring of the woman. In light of this, Peter's word to us is: "Resist him, firm in your faith, knowing that the same kinds of suffering are being experienced by your brotherhood throughout the world" (1 Pet. 5:9). The reality is that Satan is a defeated foe.

Ever since the garden, God has purposed Satan's existence and opposition to fulfill his divine plan for his people. But that perfect plan of God's includes a future day of doom for the Devil. There is a day coming when Satan's tail will no longer be whipping through the lives of God's people. John saw this day in advance and recorded what he saw in Revelation: "The devil who had deceived them was thrown into the lake of fire and sulfur where the beast and the false prophet were, and they will be tormented day and night forever and ever" (Rev. 20:10). All the offspring of the Serpent will be forever bound, far, far away from the offspring of the woman who will have made their home in the New Jerusalem. "Nothing unclean will ever enter it, nor anyone who does what is detestable or false, but only those who are written in the Lamb's book of life" (Rev. 21:27). The list of names written in this book is a list we'll never get bored with or want to skip or skim through.

The Protection of the Offspring of the Woman

Our confident hope in this coming day of judgment for Satan and his offspring enables us to make sense of the seemingly inflated promises of protection found in Psalm 91. Psalm 91 does promise the Lord's protection. The protection promised here to those who take refuge in God is protection from the destruction that will fall on the Serpent and his offspring on judgment day. The psalmist describes that day in verses 7–8:

> A thousand may fall at your side,
>> ten thousand at your right hand,
>> but it will not come near you.
> You will only look with your eyes
>> and see the recompense of the wicked.

By inspiration of the Holy Spirit, the psalmist looks into the future to see the day when "the wicked" get their due. And by "the wicked," we don't mean simply people who do bad things. The wicked are all who, instead of being at enmity with the Serpent, are in league with him, all who have refused to be reconciled to God. The picture presented in verses 7 and 8 is that of those who dwell "in the shelter of the Most High" (v. 1), watching as the offspring of the Serpent finally get what is coming to them. The promise of Psalm 91, presented to those who have found their refuge in God, is that they will be protected from all the punishments experienced by those in league with the Devil. The promise of this psalm is not wholesale physical protection in this life from everything that might threaten our comfort, but protection from the judgment that is ultimately going to fall on the Serpent and his offspring.

So beginning in verse 3 (and it will be helpful to have your Bible open to Psalm 91, or refer to it in the introduction of this chapter, to trace your way through this argument), when the psalmist says, "He will deliver you from the snare of the fowler / and from the deadly pestilence," we're meant to understand that while the offspring of the Serpent will be caught in this snare and afflicted by this deadly pestilence, those who put their trust in God will be safe. We will be protected by God, according to verses 5 and 6, from the terror, the arrow, the pestilence, and the destruction that will be experienced by the wicked. When we get to verses 9 and 10, we see that while evil will fall, and a plague will come down on all who have made their home with the Evil One, all who have made the Lord their dwelling place will find refuge in him.

The promise in verses 12 and 13 is that angels will keep you from striking your foot against a stone and getting your heel bruised. In fact, it promises that "the serpent you will trample underfoot." Because we know the story of the offspring, it is here that we begin to make the connection. There will be no bruising of our heels on this day because Christ will have taken all that bruising upon himself at the cross. He suffered the deadly pestilence. He was pierced by the arrows of judgment. He experienced utter destruction at noonday. Even though he was perfectly good, all our evil was allowed to fall on him. At the cross we see Jesus experience the recompense that wicked people like you and me really deserve.

According to verses 14–16, all who hold fast to Christ in love will be delivered, protected, rescued, honored, satisfied, and saved. But this is possible only because Christ was not delivered; he was not rescued. Jesus was not protected so that you and I will be protected forever.

So now when I read Psalm 91, instead of being resentful that somehow God has failed to protect me or my family, I can see that Christ has provided ultimate protection. I am sheltered in the shadow of the Almighty, and nothing can ultimately harm me. Everything promised in Psalm 91 will be mine on the day when judgment falls. When I call to him, he will answer me. He will be with me in trouble. He will rescue me. With long life he will satisfy me and show me his salvation.

And I can now see that God did not, in fact, withhold his promised protection from my children, Hope and Gabriel. He never promised that they would never face danger or death in this life. But he has promised to gather his own to himself, where he will protect them from ultimate and eternal harm. Hope and Gabe are now experiencing this satisfaction and salvation in a far more vivid way than I do. They're protected. They're safe. And I can rest in that. I find peace in that. And I can wait for all God's promises of protection to be fulfilled on the day he returns and calls me and Hope and Gabe and all who are his to life.[5]

As the reality of the story of the offspring of the woman and the offspring of the Serpent works its way through our thinking and our emotions, it has the power to fill us with courage to face the worst the world has to sling at us. We begin to see that even though we might lose our lives, we will not—in fact, cannot—ultimately perish.

My friend, you have an enemy. He's against you. But God is for you, and nothing can separate you from him. If you are in Christ, you are absolutely secure. Whosoever believes in him *will not perish*. Does that mean you won't ever be harmed in this life? Does that mean you won't face death? No. It means that even though you die, you won't ultimately perish. It means that even if terrorists come to get you, or an evil regime seeks to starve you, or an interrogator threatens to torture you, they cannot ultimately destroy you. It means that while Satan might win a battle or two in your life, he cannot and will not win the battle for your soul. He cannot have you as his own for eternity.

The day will come when Jesus's victory over Satan will become the shared victory of all who are joined to him. Until then, we hold on to the promise: "The God of peace will soon crush Satan under your feet" (Rom. 16:20). Until then we say, "Come quickly, Lord Jesus. Come and destroy the Serpent for good. Come and gather your people safely to yourself in a place forever secure, a home even better than Eden." Until then we sing:

> A mighty fortress is our God;
> a bulwark never failing.
> Our helper, He amid the flood
> of mortal ills prevailing.
> For still our ancient foe

doth seek to work us woe;
His craft and pow'r are great,
and, armed with cruel hate,
On earth is not his equal.

Did we in our own strength confide,
our striving would be losing,
Were not the right Man on our side,
the Man of God's own choosing:
Dost ask who that may be?
Christ Jesus, it is He;
Lord Sabaoth, His name,
from age to age the same,
And He must win the battle.

And though this world, with devils filled,
should threaten to undo us,
We will not fear, for God hath willed
His truth to triumph through us;
The Prince of Darkness grim,
we tremble not for him;
His rage we can endure,
for lo, his doom is sure,
One little word shall fell him.

That word above all earthly pow'rs,
no thanks to them, abideth;
The Spirit and the gifts are ours
through Him who with us sideth;
Let goods and kindred go,
this mortal life also;
The body they may kill:
God's truth abideth still,
His kingdom is forever.[6]

8

The Story of a Dwelling Place

When I got my first job in Waco, Texas, I decided that I'd rather live alone than with roommates, which meant that I had to find a very cheap place to live. I ended up living on one side of an old duplex and paid the landlady seventy-five dollars a month for the pleasure. I loved living there by myself—at least until David and I got engaged and he moved into what was going to be our first apartment on Alford Drive. We called it Avocadoland. This was 1986, and everything in it was 1960s or '70s avocado—from the shag carpet to the countertops to the entryway light fixture. And we loved it. Because it was home. Once David had moved into the apartment a couple of months before our wedding, it became all I could do to get into my car at night and drive back to my little duplex. I loved him, and I just wanted to be at home, in our home, together.

We've lived in a number of places since Avocadoland. And today as I write, there's a "For Sale" sign in our front yard. We've lived in our current house for over twenty years and experienced a lot of life within these walls. But David's growing business requires more space these days,[1] so we're moving to a house a few blocks away that will be better suited to our life and work. Interestingly we find ourselves far more particular about carpet and light fixtures and countertops thirty years after Avocadoland made us so very happy. But, really, we know that the same thing that made us happy on Alford Drive will make us happy in this new house—being at home, in our home, together.

This desire we all have to be at home with those we love must be one aspect of being made in God's image, because the story of the Bible is the story of God working out his plan to be at home with his people. The great passion of God's heart, as revealed from Genesis to Revelation, is to be at home with his people in a place where nothing can separate or alienate or contaminate, enjoying a face-to-face relationship of pure joy with no goodbyes. In fact, one of the most amazing things about the story we read in the Bible is that it is much more about God's desire to dwell with his people than about his people's desire to dwell with him. Doesn't that seem a bit upside down? Shouldn't we be the ones who have a desperate desire to live in his presence?

Yes, many of us have a longing to be relieved of living in this sin-sick world. But I'm not sure that is the same thing as having a longing to be at home with God. Many of us would have to admit that our relationship with God is not nearly as passionate as we might wish, and our desire to be with him isn't as strong as it ought to be. We sometimes find that we want to keep God at a safe distance. We might like to have him settle into the guesthouse out back so he's nearby when we need him, but we don't really want him close enough to be in our business. Fortunately, the Bible clearly reveals that God's intentions cannot be thwarted by a lack of passion on the part of his people. The story of human history is a story of God's ongoing intention to make his home with us in spite of our fluctuating inclinations to find our home in him.

At Home with His People in Eden

"In the beginning, God created the heavens and the earth" as a sanctuary filled with goodness where he intended to dwell with his people.[2] God furnished his home with colorful blooming plants and nourished it with babbling streams and flooded it with radiant light shining out of blue sky. (Maybe there was even an avocado tree or two somewhere in there.) It was his intention that the garden would spread so that the whole of the earth would become a home he would share with his image bearers. But then Adam and Eve, in effect, threw out the welcome mat for an invader, the Serpent, and let him make himself at home in God's home.

We read in Genesis 3:8 that Adam and Eve "heard the sound of the LORD God walking in the garden in the cool of the day." It might sound as though God was taking his regular leisurely afternoon stroll in the garden and was caught by surprise when he encountered the rebellion that had developed in his absence. But that's not what happened. Your Bible may offer an alternative translation to "in the cool of day," because the Hebrew words could also be translated "in the "wind" or "in the "spirit" of the day. So perhaps we should understand that Adam and Eve heard God coming in the spirit of "the day," or coming in the spirit of judgment day.[3] Throughout the Bible we read about "the day" or "the day of the Lord" when God will come in judgment and salvation. Clearly this day in Eden was the first of one of those days. This was judgment day, which for Adam and Eve meant that it was also eviction day. No longer could they live in the holy sanctuary of Eden in the presence of a holy God, because they had become unholy people.

But God's intention to dwell with a holy people in a holy land could not be thwarted by human sin. Instead, God began working out his plan to make it possible for sinners to be made clean and holy in order to live in his presence. God told Abraham to leave his home and his family to go make a new home in a new land (Gen. 12:3). "So [Abraham] built there an altar to the LORD, who had appeared to him. From there he moved to the hill country on the east of Bethel and pitched his tent" (Gen. 12:7–8). Abraham built an altar, a mini sanctuary, at this place where God appeared to him at Bethel, a name that means "house of God." The Bible is developing a pattern that connects God's presence to fire and sacrifice and home.

Later, God appeared to Abraham again and made a covenant "to be God to you and to your offspring after you. And I will give to you and to your offspring after you the land of your sojournings, all the land of Canaan, for an everlasting possession, and I will be their God" (Gen. 17:7–8). God was saying, *We're going to be bound together forever through an everlasting covenant. And at the heart of this covenant is relationship. I'm going to be God to you.* Do you hear the intimacy? God is not simply saying that he is going to be God to the world in a general way, even though he is God to the whole world. He's getting personal. *I'm going to be God to you, and I'm going to provide a home for you where we can work out this relationship together.*

God reiterated this promise to Abraham's son, Isaac, when he appeared to him, saying, "'I am the God of Abraham your father. Fear not, for I am with you and will bless you and multiply your offspring for my servant Abraham's sake.' So [Isaac] built an altar there and called upon the name of the LORD and pitched his tent there" (Gen. 26:24–25). Isaac wanted to live as close as possible to the place where God had visited him. So he pitched his tent there. A generation later, Isaac's son Jacob also built an altar, establishing a mini sanctuary at the same place where his grandfather Abraham had experienced God's presence on earth (Gen. 35:3).

A generation later, however, Jacob's sons found themselves in Egypt, far away from the home that God had promised to Abraham, Isaac, and Jacob. God sent his people a deliverer to bring them out of Egypt and lead them to the home he intended to share with them. God came down to lead and protect them in a pillar of cloud by day and a pillar of fire by night. Whenever they wondered if God cared about them, they could look up in the sky and see his presence in the pillar of cloud and fire. God led them safely across the Red Sea to the foot of Mount Sinai and invited Moses up the mountain to meet with him. There on the mountain, God provided Moses with blueprints for a home, a tent, in which he intended to come down and dwell among his people. While in the past he had appeared to Abraham and Isaac and Jacob and Moses from time to time, God intended to move into the neighborhood. He wanted a more permanent presence among his people. He wanted to be at the center of their camp and, more significantly, at the center of their lives.

At Home among His People in the Wilderness

"Let them make me a sanctuary," God told Moses, "that I may dwell in their midst. Exactly as I show you concerning the pattern of the tabernacle, and of all its furniture, so you shall make it" (Ex. 25:8–9). Since the Israelites were living in tents in the wilderness, and Yahweh desired to dwell among his people, he too intended to live in a tent. This tent, or tabernacle, was to be built to the very detailed specifications God provided. The writer of Hebrews says that the tabernacle, and later the temple, were "copies of the true things" (Heb. 9:24) and "a shadow of the good things to come" (Heb. 10:1). This tent was intended to serve as a reminder or replica of the home God once shared with his people in Eden. At the same time, it provided a preview of the home God intends to share with his people in the new heaven and the new earth and the way he would make it possible for them to live in his presence. In the details of the tabernacle's design, we see a reflection of the paradise of Eden as well as an architectural model of Eden 2.0.

Just as the original creation had three parts—Eden, where God's presence was experienced; a larger garden adjacent to Eden that was watered by rivers flowing out of Eden (Gen. 2:10); and undeveloped land that Adam and Eve and their offspring were meant to eventually inhabit—so the tabernacle was divided into three main parts. There was an inner room, called the "Most Holy Place" or the "Holy of Holies," where God would dwell. Adjacent was an outer room, which was called the "holy place," where the priests served. Surrounding this was a courtyard where ordinary Israelites could gather to offer their sacrifices.[4]

The Most Holy Place, as the room where God would dwell on earth, was designed as an outpost of heaven. The psalmist put it this way: "He built his sanctuary like the high heavens, / like the earth, which he has founded forever" (Ps. 78:69). The colors used reflected the blue of the sky and the royalty of the great King who dwelt there. The pure gold overlay that went into every crevice pictured the glory of God that radiates into every corner of heaven. The heart of the room—the ark of the covenant—reflected the heart of God himself. The ark contained the stone tablets on which the Ten Commandments were engraved, commandments that reflect his character. The ark of the covenant was covered by the mercy seat, or atonement cover, which demonstrated his provision for sinners—mercy and atonement. Once a year the high priest would pass through the heavy curtain that separated this room, the Most Holy Place, from the holy place and would sprinkle the blood of an animal sacrifice on the mercy seat. In this way, God would see the blood of an atoning sacrifice and be satisfied (Ex. 25:10–22).

In the outer room, the holy place, there was to be a table to hold the bread of the Presence, a lampstand to provide light, and an altar on which a priest would burn incense every morning and night (Ex. 25:23–40; 30:1–10). In the courtyard surrounding the tent would be the bronze altar on which priests would offer sacrifices and the bronze basin used by the priests for ceremonial cleansing (Ex. 27:1; 30:18).

The bdellium and onyx stones used in the design of the tabernacle were the same precious stones found in Eden (Gen. 2:12). The lampstand was designed to look like a flowering tree, similar to the tree of life in Eden. The image of two cherubim was woven into the curtain as if guarding the throne of God, just as two cherubim guarded the entrance to Eden. But, most significantly, just as God had met with his people in Eden, God now promised, "I will dwell among the people of Israel and will be their God. And they shall know that I am the LORD their God, who brought them out of the land of Egypt that I might dwell among them. I am the LORD their God" (Ex. 29:45–46).

A life quite literally built around the tabernacle would hopefully keep the people's hearts engaged in anticipation of the day when God would live among them, not shrouded in the tent and approached by the high priest only once a year, but in a more approachable and intimate way. Hopefully the ongoing sacrifice of bulls and goats and lambs would instill in his people a longing for God's once-for-all sacrifice that would be so valuable, so perfect, and so thoroughly acceptable that animal sacrifice would come to an end. Hopefully the limited access to his presence in the tabernacle would fill them with longing for the day when they would be able, with confidence, to draw near to the throne of grace, to receive mercy and find grace to help in time of need (Heb. 4:16).

When the work of the tabernacle was completed according to the blueprint God provided, "the cloud covered the tent of meeting, and the glory of the LORD filled the tabernacle" (Ex. 40:34). They could visibly see the presence of God in the fiery cloud that came down over the tabernacle. But the people of God had to remain at a distance. They were confined to the outer court, excluded from the tabernacle itself, which could be entered only by the priests. God was among his people, yet still out of reach for ordinary believers.

God remained among his people in the tabernacle throughout the forty years that they made their home in a very inhospitable place— the wilderness. And when the day came that they were finally ready to move into their more permanent home in Canaan, Moses told them to be on the lookout for the place where God could make his more permanent home among them there. Moses told them, "But you shall seek the place that the LORD your God will choose out of all your tribes to put his name and make his habitation there" (Deut. 12:5).

At Home among His People in the Temple

It was five hundred years later when King David finally saw the place. The Lord instructed him to build an altar on the threshing floor of Ornan the Jebusite. When he presented burnt offerings and peace offerings there, the Lord answered him with fire from heaven (1 Chronicles 21). David had experienced the Lord's presence with him ever since he was a boy out watching his father's sheep, but not like this—not visibly in the form of fire. Experiencing God's presence in this way convinced him that this was the place to build a house for God (1 Chron. 22:1).

David had built a beautiful palace for himself in Jerusalem, and it made no sense to him that the great King, for whom he was merely a vice-regent, would live in a tent—the tabernacle that had been built for him five hundred years earlier. So David determined that he would build a house for God. Surely his motives were good, but he was getting ahead of God. God said to David through the prophet Nathan:

> I have not lived in a house since the day I brought up Israel to this day, but I have gone from tent to tent and from dwelling to dwelling. In all places where I have moved with all Israel, did I speak a word with any of the judges of Israel, whom I commanded to shepherd my people, saying, "Why have you not built me a house of cedar?" (1 Chron. 17:5–6)

As long as his people were wandering, which they had done for many years in the wilderness and were still doing as they continued to take possession of the land in Israel, God intended to wander with them. Not until all their enemies had been defeated and his people were settled and secure would God be ready to move out of the traveling tent and into a permanent home. David was to continue subduing the enemies of Israel, while it would fall to his son Solomon to build the temple.

David, however, did begin collecting all the materials necessary to build the temple. He organized the Levites, the priests, the musicians, the gatekeepers, the treasurers, and other officials. (When you see how many chapters in the Bible are devoted to building the tabernacle and temple and staffing it and everything surrounding it, do you not get the sense that the place where God intended to dwell among his people is a really big deal to him?) "Then David gave Solomon his son the plan of the vestibule of the temple, and of its houses, its treasuries, its upper rooms, and its inner chambers, and of the room for the mercy seat; and the plan of all that he had in mind for the courts of the house of the LORD" (1 Chron. 28:11–12). David explained, "All this he made clear to me in writing from the hand of the LORD, all the work to be done according to the plan" (1 Chron. 28:19). Just as Moses had received the plan or pattern for the tabernacle from God, so David received the plans for the temple, which had the same rooms, shape, and furniture as the tabernacle, as a revelation from God.

We read in 2 Chronicles 3:1, "Then Solomon began to build the house of the LORD in Jerusalem on Mount Moriah, where the LORD had appeared to David his father, at the place that David had appointed, on the threshing floor of Ornan the Jebusite." The threshing floor David purchased to build the temple was on Mount Moriah, where God had come down to meet Abraham and had provided a ram to sacrifice in place of Abraham's son. This was the place where God came down in fire and accepted David's sacrifice. When the temple was built, it became the place where God came down to accept the sacrifices of God's people in a much bigger and ongoing way. This was like no other building project or process in the history of house building. All the stones were prepared at the quarry so that "neither hammer nor axe nor any tool of iron was heard in the house while it was being built" (1 Kings 6:7). This holy house went up in a holy hush over seven years.

When Israelites walked into the temple, it took them back—back to the beauty of the house God had built so long ago, that initial outpost of heaven, the garden of Eden. The temple in Jerusalem had gourds and open flowers carved into its cedar walls; pomegranates carved in its latticework; two cherubim made of wood with wings spread out seemingly on guard over the Most Holy Place; a basin made to look like a lily; lampstands made to look like trees with branches; and the veil woven with blue, purple, and crimson fabrics—all of it overlaid with sparkling gold. But it also pointed forward to something God would do in the future to enable his people to be at home with him again, a day when heaven would come down to earth so that earth will become heaven.[5]

When the work was complete, the people gathered for a dedication, and the ark of the covenant was put into its place in the inner sanctuary of the temple. "And when the priests came out of the Holy Place, a cloud filled the house of the LORD, so that the priests could not stand to minister because of the cloud, for the glory of the LORD filled the house of the LORD" (1 Kings 8:10–11). Solomon said to God, "I have indeed built you an exalted house, a place for you to dwell in forever" (v. 13). Solomon longed for the temple to be the place on earth where God's presence would be found. "The LORD our God be with us, as he was with our fathers," he prayed (1 Kings 8:57).

And God answered that prayer. God was with his people in the Most Holy Place of the temple. But over time his people took his presence there for granted. The kingdom became divided, and the northern kingdom built their own "temple" in Samaria. The kings in Judah went back and forth in regard to reverence for the temple. Things took a decided turn for the worse when King Manasseh built altars to pagan gods, not just in the hills surrounding the city, but right in the temple! (2 Kings 21:4–6). When we consider the care God took to assure the holiness and purity of his dwelling place, that should make us feel a bit sick. And then, just when we think it can't get worse, we read that in 597 BC, when Nebuchadnezzar of Babylon captured Jerusalem, "the king of Babylon . . . carried off all the treasures of the house of the LORD and the treasures of the king's house, and cut in pieces all the vessels of gold in the temple of the LORD" (2 Kings 24:12–13). All the beautiful objects of the dwelling place of the one true God were cut apart and carted off to be used in the temples to Nebuchadnezzar's false gods (see Ezra 1:7).

The prophet Ezekiel was already an exile in Babylon when news of the destruction of the temple reached him. He was a man who loved God's house and had intended to spend his life working there as a priest, so this news devastated him. In a vision he saw this: "the glory of the LORD went up from the cherub to the threshold of the house, and the house was filled with the cloud, and the court was filled with the brightness of the glory of the LORD" (Ezek. 10:4). When we are in our home and walk to the threshold, what are we doing? We're leaving. Ezekiel saw the glory of God moving toward the door to leave the temple he loved.[6] But then in his vision he saw the glory of God moving east—in the direction of the exiles in Babylon! The God who loves to dwell with his people was moving in the direction of his people, saying, "I will be a sanctuary to them" (see Ezek. 11:16). The real sanctuary of God, the place where the people of God, including you and me, find our home, is not where the masonry is but where God is. Surely this is what Moses meant in Psalm 90:1 when he declared,

"Lord, *you* have been our dwelling place in all generations." We're beginning to understand through this story of the Bible that our longing for home is a longing not for a place but for a person.

Later, Ezekiel was given the vision of a future temple. The dimensions of this temple were given to Ezekiel not in feet or inches but in miles. That's interesting. Clearly this temple will be of much greater scale than the former temple in Jerusalem. He saw in his vision the tangible, visible glory of God arriving from the east, from the direction of the exiles in Babylon, to inhabit this new temple. The altar, the priests, the feasts and festivals, and the offerings and sacrifices in his vision of this new temple seem similar to the previous temple, but there are dramatic differences that cause us to think that Ezekiel is seeing not an architectural temple in the historical city of Jerusalem but rather a spiritual temple that will define the New Jerusalem. Ezekiel describes water flowing out of this temple. Everywhere the river flows becomes fresh and alive again. Ezekiel sees it transforming the world as the blessing of God pours out from this new temple to the ends of the earth. On the banks of the river are trees. Ezekiel writes, "Their leaves will not wither, nor their fruit fail, but they will bear fresh fruit every month, because the water for them flows from the sanctuary. Their fruit will be for food, and their leaves for healing" (Ezek. 47:12). And we see something familiar as we read it. It looks like the garden of Eden all over again, except even better. Ezekiel seems to be describing the living water of the gospel flowing out from Jerusalem to every nation. It seems like what we read about in Revelation 21 and 22, the new garden-city temple, and we realize that the temple Ezekiel saw in his vision is none other than the new heaven and the new earth.

When God's people were allowed to return to Jerusalem under the leadership of Ezra and Nehemiah, they began rebuilding the temple, but they got distracted. God spoke to them through his prophet Haggai, encouraging them to continue the work. God promised through Haggai, "I will shake all nations, so that the treasures of all nations shall come in, and I will fill this house with glory. . . . The latter glory of this house shall be greater than the former, says the LORD of hosts. And in this place I will give peace, declares the LORD of hosts" (Hag. 2:7–9).

Later God spoke through the prophet Malachi, promising, "The Lord whom you seek will suddenly come to his temple; and the messenger of the covenant in whom you delight, behold, he is coming, says the LORD of hosts" (Mal. 3:1). But there was no sign of the Lord coming to their rebuilt temple. There was no cloud, no fire, no appearances of God's presence. About two hundred years later one of Alexander the Great's successors decided to abolish the Jews' ancestral worship, and for three years the Jerusalem temple was given over to the worship of a Greek divinity, which the Jews called "the abomination of desolation." Then, in 19 BC, Herod, a ruler over Israel put in place by Rome, went to work to rebuild the broken-down temple once again.

At Home among His People in Jerusalem

It was to Herod's temple that Mary and Joseph took their eight-day-old son. The Lord whom God's people had so long sought suddenly came to his temple. Simeon, a man who had spent his lifetime looking for the Lord to come to his temple, saw the baby and recognized him that day (Luke 2:25–33). Twelve years later Jesus traveled to Jerusalem with his parents and lingered at the temple. His panicked parents found him sitting among the teachers, listening and asking questions. He seemed perfectly at home, asking his parents, "Why were you looking for me? Did you not know that I must be in my Father's house?" (Luke 2:49).

Immanuel, God with us, had come to dwell among his people. In John we read, "The Word became flesh and dwelt among us, and we have seen his glory" (John 1:14). Once again the glory of God had descended to dwell (or, to use John's actual Greek word, to "tabernacle") among his people. This time he came not in the form of cloud and fire but in flesh and blood.

Jesus taught in the temple and healed in the temple and drove out the moneychangers from the temple. When the Jews questioned his authority for doing so, he said, "Destroy this temple, and in three days I will raise it up" (John 2:19). That was confusing to everyone who heard it, since its ten thousand workers had been at work for forty-six years to rebuild it. John explains what Jesus meant: "He was speaking about the temple of his body. When therefore he was raised from the dead, his disciples remembered that he had said this, and they believed the Scripture and the word that Jesus had spoken" (John 2:21–22). It wasn't until after Jesus's resurrection that they could see that the building they had sought as home over the centuries had been merely a shadow of their true home, the true temple, the person of Jesus Christ.

But not everyone saw this so clearly. Instead of celebrating that the glory of God had come down in the person of Jesus, the rulers of the temple conspired to crucify the Lord of glory (1 Cor. 7:8). But the crucifixion of Jesus was not merely the result of a human plot against him; it was, most profoundly, the result of an eternal, divine covenant of redemption made between Father and Son. On the cross, zeal for his Father's house—for his Father's plan to make his home with redeemed sinners like you and me—consumed him, crushed him, killed him. On the cross, the true temple was destroyed, even as the Great High Priest offered the perfect sacrifice. And in just three days the true temple was raised, never to be destroyed again.

Once the sacrifice was offered, the veil that had hung between the holy place and the Most Holy Place in the temple in Jerusalem split from top to bottom, a dramatic tearing down of the barrier between God and his people, opening a new way for God to dwell among—even in—his people.[7] God hadn't been present in the Most Holy Place in the temple for a long time, and with the tearing of the veil it became clear that that era and expectation were over for good. Once sin had been fully and finally atoned for in the death of Christ, God threw open the doors to welcome not just the high priest, and not just those born into the priestly tribe, and not even just those who were born into a Jewish home, but people from every tribe, tongue, and nation who wanted to dwell in the presence of God, having been made holy by the blood of Christ.

At Home in His People on Earth

Prior to his death, the disciples had been troubled when Jesus began to speak to them about his departure. But Jesus told them that it would actually be *better* for them that he go, because then God's presence would dwell not just *among* them, but *in* them. Imagine what it must have been like for these disciples, whose whole lives had centered on the temple, to be told that they no longer needed to long for the visible presence of God to descend once again on the temple in Jerusalem. Instead, God would descend on them individually and corporately and remain there throughout the whole of their lives.

That's exactly what happened on the day of Pentecost. About 120 of those who had put their faith in Christ were gathered together when they thought they heard the sound of wind blowing. In fact, it was God breathing on them. Then they saw fire, which they recognized as a symbol of God's presence, but this fire didn't rest on a bush or a mountain or over a tent as it had in Moses's day, or on the temple as it had in Solomon's day. This fire came to rest on people. God was demonstrating in a visual way the reality of his presence coming to dwell *in* them. They were just beginning to understand that they had become living, breathing, walking, talking temples in which God dwelt by his Spirit.

If you have become joined to Christ by faith, you too are part of a living, breathing, walking, talking temple in which God dwells by his Spirit. Peter writes that we are living stones that are being built up as a spiritual house (1 Pet. 2:5). And Paul writes that we are "being built together into a dwelling place for God by the Spirit" (Eph. 2:19–22). God is, indeed, working out his plan to dwell with his people.

Living water is flowing from the temple as the gospel is proclaimed and embraced and lives are healed and made whole, just as Ezekiel saw in his vision of the new temple. God is even now building his new temple, the church, not with limestone hewn from quarries in the Middle East, but with living stones, the lives of ordinary believers like you and me.

Even as God dwells in us by his Spirit, we continue to long for the day when we will relate to God face-to-face. "Now [we] know in part; then [we] shall know fully, even as [we] have been fully known" (1 Cor. 13:12). Sometimes the loneliness and difficulty of life in this world are overwhelming, and we just want to go home. We would rather be away from the body and at home with the Lord (2 Cor. 5:8). We are seeking a homeland (Heb. 11:14). We've heard the promise: "I go to prepare a place for you. . . . And if I go and prepare a place for you, I will come again and will take you to myself, that where I am you may be also" (John 14:2–3). And we are ready to go.

And yet we also have to admit that there are times when our hearts really aren't set on that home. Sometimes we are so tied to this world, so enamored by it, so invested in it, that we yawn at the promise of being at home with God.

The good news of the gospel is that Jesus showed the true zeal for God's house that we often lack. His zeal has been credited to our spiritual account. At the cross Jesus took upon himself the punishment we deserve for our self-centered focus on our own houses—building them, decorating them, furnishing them, cleaning them, living in them—while having a paltry passion for his Father's house. The good news of the gospel is that God will be faithful to his commitment to come and dwell with us, his people, even though our desire to dwell with him often wavers or fades.

The day is coming when we'll hear a loud voice from the throne saying, "Behold, the dwelling place of God is with man. He will dwell with them, and they will be his people, and God himself will be with them as their God" (Rev. 21:3). We'll finally be at home, together—no more relating to God from a distance, no more being estranged from him because of our sin. We will feel and know the closeness of God like never before. There is no chance that we'll be evicted. We will live with the One who knows us intimately and loves us perfectly. His desire to dwell with us will have been satisfied, and all that is lacking in our desire to dwell with him will have been provided. Our hearts will have caught up to his so that we will be fully at home in his presence.

Until then, we keep on seeking to turn our heart toward home by using the divinely provided words of the psalms. Whenever we're tempted to think that the pleasures of this world will satisfy us, we say:

> You make known to me the path of life;
>> in your presence there is fullness of joy;
>> at your right hand are pleasures forevermore. (Ps. 16:11)

Whenever guilt over our sin weighs so heavy that we begin to wonder if there's a place for us in the home God is preparing, we say:

> Surely goodness and mercy shall follow me
>> all the days of my life,
> and I shall dwell in the house of the Lord
>> forever. (Ps. 23:6)

Whenever we find ourselves seeking after things that leave us empty, we discipline our desires by saying:

> One thing have I asked of the Lord,
>> that will I seek after:
> that I may dwell in the house of the Lord
>> all the days of my life,
> to gaze upon the beauty of the Lord
>> and to inquire in his temple. (Ps. 27:4)

When we find our heart cold toward the things of God and the place where we will dwell with him forever, we fan the flames of longing in our heart by saying,

> How lovely is your dwelling place,
>> O Lord of hosts!
> My soul longs, yes, faints
>> for the courts of the Lord;
> my heart and flesh sing for joy
> to the living God. (Ps. 84:1–2)

And we keep on singing about the home we will share with our God forever:

Our God, our help in ages past,
our hope for years to come,
our shelter from the stormy blast,
and our eternal home.

Under the shadow of your throne
your saints have dwelt secure;
sufficient is your arm alone,
and our defense is sure.

Before the hills in order stood
or earth received its frame,
from everlasting you are God,
to endless years the same.

A thousand ages in your sight
are like an evening gone,
short as the watch that ends the night
before the rising sun.

Time, like an ever-rolling stream,
soon bears us all away;
we fly forgotten, as a dream
dies at the opening day.

Our God, our help in ages past,
our hope for years to come,
still be our guard while troubles last,
and our eternal home![8]

9

The Story of the City

The *Telegraph* of London recently published its annual list of the best cities to live in, along with the reasons each city is so livable.[1] The list includes:

- Stockholm, Sweden, the cleanest capital city according to World Health Organization pollution statistics.
- Melbourne, Australia, a moody, complex, deep-thinking metropolis obsessed with art, food, and coffee.
- Berlin, Germany, where parties can go on for days rather than hours.
- Amsterdam, Netherlands, which combines its glittering past with a wry, rough, rebellious contemporary edginess.
- Vancouver, British Columbia, where everyone's happy— no Ontario blizzards, no Los Angeles smog, no Hong Kong chaos. Just mountains, sea, big skies, and wide streets.

- Zurich, Switzerland, where the streets are clean and the trams run on time.

Number one on their list, which they describe as the most livable place in the world, is Vienna, Austria. They call it a city that charms and seduces from scratch, but even more, the longer you stay, a seemingly never-ending wealth of things to do and see.

I'm sure these cities are wonderful. I'd like to visit every one of them. But when I snooped around on the Internet, I found some interesting things about these cities that this article didn't mention.

Yes, Stockholm, Sweden, is a clean city, but the number of Swedish women who say they have been the victims of sexual assault of some kind in the past year is on the rise. Yes, Melbourne, Australia, may be a deep-thinking metropolis, but fear of terrorism, specifically vehicle attacks, has meant that concrete bollards were recently installed in nine major public spaces. Yes, Berlin, Germany, may have parties that go on for days, but an influx of refugees at the rate of four hundred a day has put Berlin on the edge of a humanitarian crisis. Yes, Amsterdam has edginess, but that edginess works its way out in the form of heavily drugged tourists walking past window after window of sex workers offering their bodies for sale. Yes, there are plenty of happy people in Vancouver, British Columbia, but there is also a lack of affordable housing and an investigation into political campaign corruption. Yes, the streets are clean in Zurich, but the defense minister recently announced that the question isn't if a terrorist attack will take place in Switzerland, but when. And even Vienna, which charms and seduces, has a problem with too many pigeons and pickpockets.

As beautiful and inviting, as culturally rich and economically vibrant as the greatest cities in the world may be, they all have an ugly underbelly. Anyone willing to open her eyes to the parts of town she avoids in any city won't be able to avoid seeing substandard housing, unjust labor practices, unemployment, and racial bigotry. Anyone who has looked into the eyes of a mother whose child has been killed by gang violence, or sat in court with a rape victim, or taught in a classroom where kids regularly arrive hungry, or stopped to have a conversation with a homeless veteran at the rescue mission, does not need to be convinced that no city lives up to its visitor's bureau's description.

Well, maybe that isn't completely true. There is one city sure to live up to all the superlatives of its description, one city that will not disappoint, one city where there is perfect justice, abundant provision, and complete security. The story of the Bible is the story of this city. But, really, the story of the Bible is the story of two cities—the city of man and the city of God. And what matters most about your story is which city you have made your home.

The City of Enoch

We don't know where Eden was. We get the sense that it was located on a mountain, since rivers flowed out of it, and the prophet Ezekiel described it as the "mountain of God" (Ezek. 28:14, 16). What is clear in the Genesis account of Eden is that the city of man, or at least the spirit of it, invaded the garden of God. The city of man is a city of greed, and Adam and Eve became greedy for more. The city of man is marked by a rejection of God's word and the shutting out of God's presence, and Adam and Eve rejected God's word and came to dread God's presence. The city of man has made an alliance with the god of this world, which is what Adam and Eve did in the garden. The city of man makes the false promise that men and women can be like gods, which is exactly the false promise the Serpent made to Eve.

When we turn the page from Genesis 3, where Adam and Eve were banished from the garden, we read in Genesis 4 the story of Cain murdering his brother, Abel, and being made "a fugitive and a wanderer on the earth" (Gen. 4:12). Cain felt the vulnerability of being on his own and was sure that whoever found him would kill him. So, in grace, God put a mark on Cain "lest any who found him should attack him" (v. 15). In grace God provided security to Cain through this mark, whatever it was. But Cain didn't believe this mark would really protect him. He didn't want anything to do with the God who gave the mark to him, so he "went away from the presence of the LORD and settled in the land of Nod, east of Eden. . . . When he built a city, he called the name of the city after the name of his son, Enoch" (vv. 16–17).

Cain didn't trust the security God provided for him, so he decided to create his own security in the form of a city. He named the city Enoch, which means "initiation" or "dedication." Cain initiated a city dedicated to his preferences, including his preference that God just stay out. There was no interest in obeying God's commands in this city—including God's command of one man being joined to one woman for life, so we're not terribly surprised to read that one of Cain's descendants took two wives (v. 19). Arts and culture and technology were being developed in this city, but something rotten was brewing there too. Genesis records one inhabitant of this city, Lamech, saying to his wives, "I have killed a man for wounding me" (v. 23). Rub this guy the wrong way and he'll kill you. Evidently, lasting security could not be found in this city of increasing violence.

In Genesis 4, the spiritual city of man takes the form of a physical city. But before the chapter concludes, we also witness the founding of the spiritual city of God. The city of God began as and continues to be not a physical city but a spiritual one. We read that Adam and Eve had a son named Seth, and that "at that time people began to call upon the name of the LORD" (Gen. 4:26). There it is—the spiritual city of God—a city built around calling upon God rather than keeping God out. A city built out of humility instead of pride, dependence instead of independence. Those who reside in this city recognize that the security and significance they need can come only from God.

The City of Babel

A few chapters later in Genesis we read, "As people migrated from the east, they found a plain in the land of Shinar and settled there. . . . Then they said, 'Come, let us build ourselves a city and a tower with its top in the heavens, and let us make a name for ourselves, lest we be dispersed over the face of the whole earth'" (Gen. 11:2–4). God had always intended the whole earth to be inhabited by people who reflect his glory and call upon him as Lord. But these people weren't spreading; they were settling in Shinar, hoping to find some security in numbers and significance in their joint project. Instead of giving glory to God, they wanted to create their own glory. But their attempt to make a name for themselves backfired. God came down and confused their language so they could no longer plot together against him. The name of that city became Babel, which means "confusion." They made a name for themselves all right, but it wasn't exactly what they had hoped for.

The City of Sodom

One of the families dispersed over the face of the earth ended up in Ur of the Chaldeans, a city in the country of Babylonia. (Babel became Babylon in the country of Babylonia.) And as we will see throughout the story of the city, God is constantly calling to his people to come out of Babylon and to make their home in the city of God. That was the case for Abraham. "Now the LORD said to Abram, 'Go from your country and your kindred and your father's house to the land that I will show you" (Gen. 12:1). The writer of Hebrews tells us:

> By faith Abraham obeyed when he was called to go out to a place that he was to receive as an inheritance. And he went out, not knowing where he was going. By faith he went to live in the land of promise, as in a foreign land, living in tents with Isaac and Jacob, heirs with him of the same promise. For he was looking forward to the city that has foundations, whose designer and builder is God. (Heb. 11:8–10)

Abraham wasn't interested in building a city to protect himself *from* God; he was looking forward to the city built *by* God. His nephew Lot, however, saw things differently. "Abram settled in the land of Canaan, while Lot settled among the cities of the valley and moved his tent as far as Sodom. Now the men of Sodom were wicked, great sinners against the LORD" (Gen. 13:12–13).

The day came when God had had enough of Sodom's wickedness. A great cry from all the victims of Sodom's poor and needy, from its victims of sexual violence and injustice, came up to God (Ezek. 16:49). Two angels went to the city, and "the men of the city, the men of Sodom, both young and old, all the people to the last man" (Gen. 19:4) demanded that the angelic visitors come out of Lot's house so that they could rape them. "As morning dawned, the angels urged Lot, saying, 'Up! Take your wife and your two daughters who are here, lest you be swept away in the punishment of the city.'" But we read that Lot lingered. Lot was very attached to Sodom. In other words, he was like us. A part of him hated the world, but a part of him loved the world and didn't want to turn away from it. Fortunately for Lot, the angelic visitors "seized him and his wife and his two daughters by the hand, the LORD being merciful to him, and they brought him out and set him outside the city" (Gen. 19:15–16). What a picture of what we need God to do for us! Unless God in his mercy takes holds of us and those we love and brings us out, we'll perish along with all the other inhabitants of the city of man.

The City of Jerusalem

In Abraham's day there was a city called Salem, which means *shalom* or "peace." A good king named Melchizedek, who was also a priest of Yahweh, ruled there (Gen. 14:18). Eventually Salem was taken over by the Jebusites, who built a wall around the city and called it Jebus (1 Chron. 11:4). When God's people were brought into the land of promise, God gave them possession of many of the cities in Canaan, but there was one city they failed to take possession of—the city of Jebus. When David became king of Israel, he needed a capital city centrally located among the twelve tribes, a city that could become a fortress to withstand attack. And Jebus was such a city.

David took the city of Jebus and renamed it Jerusalem. It became the city in which the king of Israel had his palace. More significantly it became the holy hill where God himself dwelt in his temple among his people. Jerusalem was meant to be a holy city, the "city of Shalom." It was meant to be a city where the people of God delighted in the presence of God in their midst rather than walling him out. It was meant to be a city focused on the glory of God's name and the spread of his rule. That's what it was intended to be. But that's not what it became.

The story of Jerusalem seems to confirm everything we've come to expect so far in the Bible's story about the city. She had her glory days. We read in 1 Kings about the glory of the city as God himself came to reside in the temple built by Solomon. We read about the Queen of Sheba coming to Jerusalem because she wanted to see for herself if all she had heard about it was true. But we also read that Solomon brought foreign wives, and with them the worship of foreign gods, into the holy city of Jerusalem. Solomon seemed to imbibe the elixir served up in the city of man as he continued to build cities for his chariots and horsemen using slave labor. He even named some of the cities he built after false gods (1 Kings 9:17–18).

Over the coming centuries, Jerusalem became thoroughly sullied by idolatry and other evils, including child sacrifice. The prophet Isaiah lamented what Jerusalem had become in his day, writing in the opening of his book:

> How the faithful city
>> has become a whore,
>> she who was full of justice!
> Righteousness lodged in her,
>> but now murderers.
> Your silver has become dross,
>> your best wine mixed with water.
> Your princes are rebels
>> and companions of thieves.
> Everyone loves a bribe
>> and runs after gifts.
> They do not bring justice to the fatherless,
>> and the widow's cause does not come to them. (Isa. 1:21–23)

The prophet Ezekiel wrote that Jerusalem became even more corrupt than Sodom (Ezek. 16:48). God had destroyed Sodom when the sin of its people became too much for him to tolerate, and likewise, God determined to destroy Jerusalem when its sin became too much to tolerate. But instead of using fire as his tool of judgment, as he did with Sodom, God determined to use a city as his means of judgment on Jerusalem.

The City of Babylon

The city God determined to use was none other than Babylon. Of course, the Babylonians and their king didn't know they were a tool in the hand of a sovereign God, being used to purify God's people. When the Babylonians marched on Jerusalem, they were just doing what those in the city of man do—exercising power and eating up anything in their way. Nebuchadnezzar carried away Jerusalem's king and all the elite of the city to Babylon. A few years later the Babylonian armies came back to Jerusalem for the remaining inhabitants. Jerusalem was burned, and the temple was destroyed.

You can almost hear the king of Babylon beating his chest when Daniel, who was one of those Jerusalemites carted off to Babylon, quotes the king, saying: "Is not this great Babylon, which I have built by my mighty power as a royal residence and for the glory of my majesty?" (Dan. 4:30). Babylon was, and continues to be, in the pages of Scripture, the arrogant, enduring, God-hating, self-loving, self-confident city of man.

The prophet Jeremiah wrote to the exiles early in their Babylonian captivity to correct the false prophets who were telling them that they wouldn't be there very long. Jeremiah told the exiles they would be there for seventy years, and he spoke to them for God, saying:

> Build houses and live in them; plant gardens and eat their produce. Take wives and have sons and daughters; take wives for your sons, and give your daughters in marriage, that they may bear sons and daughters; multiply there, and do not decrease. But seek the welfare of the city where I have sent you into exile, and pray to the LORD on its behalf, for in its welfare you will find your welfare. (Jer. 29:5–7)

They were going to be there for a while, so while they lived in the city of man, they needed to live ordinary lives, planting gardens and getting married and having children. And supremely they needed to pray for the welfare of the city. They were to immerse themselves in God's Word, not the word of the false prophets among them or the indoctrination of Babylon. In this way they would be building God's alternative spiritual city in the midst of the city of man. They would be, as Jesus put it centuries later, salt and light, a city on a hill (Matt. 5:13–14). The people of God in the midst of the city of man are called not to be separate but to be distinctly different from its other inhabitants.

They also needed to live in anticipation of being delivered from Babylon. God had a future for them beyond life by the Chebar canal on the outskirts of a pagan city. The Lord said to them through his prophet Jeremiah,

> When seventy years are completed for Babylon, I will visit you, and I will fulfill to you my promise and bring you back to this place. For I know the plans I have for you, declares the LORD, plans for welfare and not for evil, to give you a future and a hope. (Jer. 29:10–11)

The promise was not that they would receive everything they hoped for during the seventy years they lived in Babylon (just as it is not a promise to us that we can expect to receive everything we hope for in the seventy or so years of our lifetime). The promise was that a future awaited them in the city of God. God himself would bring them there. Their hope and their future was that they would be delivered from Babylon and replanted in the city of God. Likewise the plans God has for us, for our welfare and not for evil, are to give us a future and a hope in his city.

Eventually, the people of God returned from exile to rebuild their temple and the city of Jerusalem. But the temple and the city were never as glorious as they had once been. They never lived up to the visions the prophets had for the city God intended for his people. Isaiah wrote about a city that was large enough to encompass the nations, where the inhabitants live in peace and righteousness with no oppression, fear, or terror (Isa. 54:2–3, 11–14). Micah wrote that in the "latter days" peoples from every nation will flow into Jerusalem, wanting to be taught the ways of God so they can walk in them. War will be gone and everyone will be provided for in a place where there is no fear (Mic. 4:1–5). Zechariah wrote of a coming day when Zion will be a place of such security and peace that young and old will be able to sit or play in its streets.[2] He wrote that people from many cities will make the city their home and enjoy God's favor and experience his presence (Zech. 8:1–8, 20–23). Ezekiel wrote, "The name of the city from that time on shall be, 'The LORD Is There'" (Ezek. 48:35).

The promises of the prophets and the songs of the psalmists about the city of God kept God's people hoping and longing for the day when God's King would come to God's city and transform it into all it was meant to be.

Jerusalem Destroyed

The day finally came when God's King did come to God's city. Readers of Luke's Gospel are made to feel the drama of his coming. In Luke 9:51 we read that Jesus "set his face to go to Jerusalem." In chapter 13 we read, "He went on his way through towns and villages, teaching and journeying toward Jerusalem" (v. 22). As he made his way, some Pharisees came to tell him that he shouldn't go to Jerusalem, because Herod wanted to kill him. Jesus responded to the warning, "I must go on my way today and tomorrow and the day following, for it cannot be that a prophet should perish away from Jerusalem" (v. 33). Do you hear the irony? While Jerusalem should have been a city that always loved and listened to God's word through God's prophets, her sad history included the rejection and even the killing of many of God's prophets (see 2 Chron. 24:20–22; Jer. 26:20–23; 38:4–6).

The greatest of all prophets, the one who doesn't just speak God's word but *is* the Word of God made flesh, was preparing to enter Jerusalem. And ever since Jesus "set his face to go to Jerusalem," going to Jerusalem had always been about going there to die. The second part of his response was not at all ironic; it was full of lament over what could have been. Jesus's heart was broken because of Jerusalem's rejection of the grace of God. "O Jerusalem, Jerusalem, the city that kills the prophets and stones those who are sent to it!" Jesus lamented. "How often would I have gathered your children together as a hen gathers her brood under her wings, and you were not willing!" (v. 34).

A short time later, as Jesus rode through the towns of Bethpage and Bethany on a colt, the people threw down their coats and blessed him as the King who comes in the name of the Lord. But when he drew near Jerusalem and saw the city, Luke writes that he wept over it (Luke 19:41). Actually, the word used for "wept" is not what we might think of as weeping—a little dabbing at the eyes as tears fall down our cheeks. The word used by Luke is closer to what we would describe as wailing, like we've seen in television footage of Middle Eastern funerals. Jesus wailed in great sorrow over the coming destruction of the city so central to God's work in the world. He wailed:

> Would that you, even you, had known on this day the things that make for peace! But now they are hidden from your eyes. For the days will come upon you, when your enemies will set up a barricade around you and surround you and hem you in on every side and tear you down to the ground, you and your children within you. And they will not leave one stone upon another in you, because you did not know the time of your visitation. (Luke 19:42–44)

Jesus was clear in these passages about why judgment was coming—rejection of God's word and rejection of God's Son. When the Roman armies of Titus came in AD 70, it wasn't merely the outworking of the imperialistic whims of the world power of the day. The armies of Titus were a tool used by God to judge his beloved city. The cause for the judgment was the city's unwillingness to be gathered together under the security provided by God, a blindness to and rejection of the reality of the presence of God in her midst during "the time of [her] visitation." The earthly city of Jerusalem was rejected by God because of her rejection of Jesus.

Jesus prepared to enter Jerusalem on a donkey, which meant that God's King was finally coming into God's city. The gates should have been flung open for him. The priests should have lined the route. Herod should have come out of his palace to bow down to the true King. Instead, Jerusalem crucified her king outside the gates of the city. Concerned for ritual purity but not genuine purity, Jerusalem didn't want to have the presence of a dead body inside the "holy city." Of course Jerusalem was not holy. In her abuse of power, her determination to keep God out, her idolatry of the temple and the law, and her confusion, Jerusalem had become Babylon.[3] It was outside the city that the pure Son of God took upon himself the corruption and oppression and self-obsession and God-rejection of the city of man. Jesus took upon himself the judgment deserved by those who have come to love the city of man, so that one day all who are willing to flee from that city to the person of Christ will be invited to make their home forever in the city of God.

Forty days after Jesus rose from the dead, the risen Jesus ascended into heaven. Ten days after that, the building of the city of God kicked into high gear. The Holy Spirit came down and reversed the curse of the ancient city of Babel. People "from every nation under heaven" (Acts 2:5) were there in Jerusalem, gathered for the feast of Pentecost. They were divided by one thing—language. But suddenly the Spirit of God came down, and the apostles began to speak with tongues of fire so that everyone heard the gospel in his own language. From the city of Jerusalem, the gospel began to spread to all Judea and Samaria and to the end of the earth. When we read the story in Acts, we see again and again that the word of God spread. Everywhere it went, it made people alive again; everywhere it went, people began to call on the name of the Lord.

And just as Jesus had said, the day soon came when the earthly city of Jerusalem was completely destroyed. Her special place within the purposes of God came to an end. Despite what many modern Christian theologies espouse about a future place for the earthly Middle Eastern city of Jerusalem in the consummation of human history,[4] once Jerusalem rejected Christ, we see in the Bible a decided turn away from the earthly Jerusalem toward the heavenly New Jerusalem.

"For here we have no lasting city, but we seek the city that is to come," the writer of Hebrews says (Heb. 13:14). "But you have come to Mount Zion and to the city of the living God, the heavenly Jerusalem" (Heb. 12:22). "The Jerusalem above is free, and she is our mother," Paul writes (Gal. 4:26).

Oh, my friend, this is the city we want to live in, the city that is to come! This is the city in which we want our roots to go deep. We want to anchor all our hopes in this city. This is the city—the only city—that will last forever.

Babylon Destroyed

In the final chapters of the Bible, it becomes clearer than ever that the Bible is the story of two cities. In these final chapters we witness the final destruction of Babylon, the city of man, as well as the long-awaited entrance of the people of God into the true and lasting city of God, the New Jerusalem.

Babylon, the city of man, is inviting in its idolatries, alluring in its beauty, intoxicating in its pleasures, and empowering in its projects. But it is also deceiving about its destiny. Its destiny is utter destruction. Christ will come again, and he will put an end to the influence of Babylon and to Babylon's persecution of God's people. All the things Babylon boasts about—her beauty, her riches, her power, her quality of life—they'll all be gone for good, melted away in the fire of God's judgment. Everything Babylon promises to people like me and you— the comfort made possible through money, the significance made possible through achievement—it will all be ripped away. Because of this coming judgment, we hear God calling to his people:

Come out of her, my people,
  lest you take part in her sins,
lest you share in her plagues. (Rev. 18:4)

Don't be fooled into thinking this passage in Revelation is directed to a future generation. This is God's call to you and me right now, today. We find ourselves living, for now, in Babylon, the city of man, but we must live here with our bags packed and our hearts set to come out of her to live forever in the city of God when we hear our true King call for us. We're called to live in the tension of being in the world but not of it. Do you feel that tension?

As strangers and exiles, we "make it clear that [we] are seeking a homeland. . . . [We] desire a better country, that is, a heavenly one. Therefore God is not ashamed to be called [our] God, for he has prepared for [us] a city" (Heb. 11:14–16). The story of the city that runs from Genesis to Revelation invites us to set our hearts on, plant our roots in, invest our lives in, and find our life in the city of God, the New Jerusalem, which will endure forever.

The New Jerusalem

An angel gave the apostle John a preview of this city. He saw "the holy city, new Jerusalem, coming down out of heaven from God" (Rev. 21:2). We won't be going back to the garden. Instead, we are headed for a garden-like city. God has taken possession of the very thing created to exclude him—the city—and he is turning it into a home for his people that will be even better than Eden.[5] Rather than being greedy for more, like Adam and Eve were, all who live in this city will be perfectly satisfied. Rather than dreading God's presence like Cain did, we'll relish it. Rather than conspiring together to defy or disobey like the inhabitants of Babel did, all the inhabitants of the New Jerusalem will conspire together on how to glorify God and enjoy him forever.

This city won't be the result of human effort; it will be the city Abraham had his heart set on, the city with foundations whose architect and builder is God. Its walls and foundations will have the names of the twelve tribes and the twelve apostles. In other words, this city will be built on the gospel promises made to the patriarchs and the gospel proclaimed by the apostles (Gal. 3:8).

The day is going to come when we will make our home in the most livable city in the world. In fact, this city will encompass the whole world (Rev. 21:12). The *tohu wabohu* will be gloriously and completely filled with radiant life and rich relationship. It will far surpass any city currently found on any list of the world's most livable cities. It will be the cleanest city anyone has ever lived in. Nothing unclean will ever enter it (Rev. 21:27). It will serve the best food and wine anyone ever ate or drank, "a feast of rich food, a feast of well-aged wine" (Isa. 25:6). Instead of parties that go on for days, the celebration will never end (Heb. 12:22). It won't just have a glittering past; it will be radiant with the glory of God into eternity future (Eph. 2:7). It won't just have no blizzards, no smog, and no chaos; it will have no tears, no death, and no night (Rev. 21:4; 22:5). The streets won't just be clean;

they'll be gold (Rev. 21:21). In this eternal city, we'll enjoy a seemingly never-ending wealth of things to do and never-ending revelations of the beauties and perfections of God.

This will be the city the psalmists sang about. In fact, look for what Psalm 87 has to say about who will inhabit this city. It's really quite surprising:

> On the holy mount stands the city he founded;
> > the LORD loves the gates of Zion
> > more than all the dwelling places of Jacob.
> Glorious things of you are spoken,
> > O city of God. *Selah*

> Among those who know me I mention Rahab and Babylon;
> > behold, Philistia and Tyre, with Cush—
> > "This one was born there," they say.
> And of Zion it shall be said,
> > "This one and that one were born in her";
> > for the Most High himself will establish her.
> The LORD records as he registers the peoples,
> > "This one was born there." *Selah* (vv. 1–6)

The psalmist is singing that the city of God will be inhabited by people who were physically born in the city of man but have been spiritually reborn in the city of God. People from Rahab, which refers to Egypt and means "arrogant one" in Hebrew, are going to walk into the city of God in humility. People from Babylon, the city of confusion, are going to become clear about who Jesus is. People from warring Philistia are going to enjoy peace with God. People from covetous Tyre are going to find their satisfaction in God. People from the remote and spiritually illiterate nation of Cush will hear the good news and run in the direction of this city to make it their home. It will be said of all whose names were recorded by God himself before the foundations of the world, "This one was born here."[6]

The day is coming when all who have taken hold of Christ will come through gates made of pearls. It won't matter if you were born in Kansas City or Toronto or Jakarta or Hong Kong or Moscow or

Nairobi or Bogotá or Sydney. You will have come away from your exile in Babylon to make your home in the New Jerusalem. Those waiting at the gate will look into the Lamb's Book of Life for your name. And when they find your name in the book, they'll point to you and say, "This one was born here." Then they'll look into your eyes and say with a shared sense of relief and joy, "Welcome home." Doesn't it make you want to sing?

> Come, we that love the Lord,
> And let our joys be known;
> Join in a song with sweet accord,
> Join in a song with sweet accord,
> And thus surround the throne
> And thus surround the throne.
> We're marching to Zion,
> Beautiful, beautiful Zion;
> We're marching upward to Zion,
> The beautiful city of God.
>
> Then let our songs abound,
> And every tear be dry;
> We're marching through Immanuel's ground
> We're marching through Immanuel's ground
> To fairer worlds on high
> To fairer worlds on high
> We're marching to Zion,
> Beautiful, beautiful Zion;
> We're marching upward to Zion,
> The beautiful city of God.[7]

Conclusion

You and I were meant to enjoy an environment, a sense of purpose and satisfaction, and an intimacy with God and each other that is even better than Adam and Eve enjoyed in Eden. Eden had the seeds of the new creation, but all those seeds will burst into glorious bloom in the new heaven and the new earth. When we enter the new Eden, our Sabbath rest, the final temple, the New Jerusalem, we'll begin to experience all that God has intended for his people all along.

🍃 While Adam and Eve became discontented with God's provision in Eden, which was a garden in the midst of a vast wilderness, those who inhabit the new creation will be perfectly content with God's vast provision in a garden-city that will extend to every corner of the earth. This means that you and I can be genuinely and increasingly contented, if not yet completely contented now.

🍃 While the tree of life in the midst of Eden held out to Adam and Eve the promise of a superior quality of life if they were obedient, the tree of life in the new creation will provide unending, abundant life and healing to all who have put their faith in the obedience of Christ. This means that the story of our lives doesn't have to be about always grabbing for the good life as we define it but about trusting God to provide a better than good life in his way and in his timing.

🍃 While Adam and Eve were made in the image and likeness of God, all who inhabit the new heaven and the new earth will have been remade in true righteousness, holiness, and knowledge, with no possibility of that image becoming marred again. This means that the story of who we are and who we will become is not ultimately being written by us. We don't have to look for a sense of identity in our appearance or our accomplishments. Instead, our identities are grounded fully in Christ and secured by who he is and what he has done.

📖 While Adam and Eve were naked and unashamed, all who are joined to Christ will be clothed in his royal righteousness and will never be vulnerable to shame again. They will be further clothed with immortality so that they will never be vulnerable to death again. This means that our stories are not all about trying to make ourselves look good. Because we know that we are being clothed in the righteousness of Christ and will awaken from death in the clothing of immortality, we don't have to be obsessed with our wardrobe now or with signs of aging. We don't have to live under the weight of shame or in the fear of death. We can trust that he is clothing us in holiness, beauty, and glory.

📖 While Adam failed and blamed his bride, our Bridegroom, Jesus, will not fail to lead his bride, the church, into a new garden-city where he will cherish this bride forever. This means that while we can desire or enjoy being loved by a human groom in this life, we don't expect that any man will love us in the ways we need most to be loved. Any man's love will be a dim shadow of being loved fully and forever by Christ.

📖 Because Adam and Eve failed in the work they were given to do in Eden, they failed to reach the seventh-day rest held out to them. But because Christ completed the work the first Adam failed to accomplish, all who are joined to him by faith will enter into unending rest with God. This means that the story of our lives doesn't have to be one breathless week after another, always trying to keep ahead of demands. The world, our families, our lives are not going to fall apart if we take time to rest in and focus on the work Christ has accomplished, and what is yet to come. As we order our lives around remembering this promised rest to come, we find that we can really rest in the here and now.

☙ While the first Adam allowed evil in the form of a serpent to invade and bring ruin to Eden, Jesus, the last Adam, has crushed the head of the ancient Serpent and will one day destroy him for good so that nothing evil will enter into the new creation. This means that the story of our lives will not be without struggle. The Enemy is against us, seeking to destroy us. But because we are joined to Christ, we know that while the Enemy may win some battles in our lives, he cannot win the war against our souls.

☙ While Adam and Eve were forced into exile from the sanctuary of Eden where they had experienced the presence of God, all who are being made pure will be welcomed into the holiness of the new temple that will cover the entire earth, where they will dwell forever in the presence of God. This means that it's not up to us to make ourselves pure enough to live in his presence. He is at work cleansing and renewing us in order to satisfy the desire of his heart, which is to dwell with his people—including you and me—forever.

☙ While Adam and Eve lived in a garden that was invaded by the city of man, all who have been reborn by the Spirit will live forever in the security and serenity of the city of God, the New Jerusalem. This means that though we find ourselves living in the city of man, which tells us its lies and tries to trap us in its allures, it doesn't define us and cannot claim us as its own. We live here as strangers and aliens. Our roots, our citizenship, and our hopes are anchored in the soil of the city of God.

This story of the Bible, my friends, is the story that has the power to change everything about your life now and into eternity future. May you find yourself in this story and its happily ever after. May you make your home, even now, in Christ, and may he one day welcome you into his eternal home that will be even better than Eden.

Discussion Guide

Following are suggested questions for group discussion. They are designed not necessarily to come to a "right" answer but to prompt deeper thinking on the topic of each chapter, encourage personal sharing in a group situation, and draw out both theological and practical implications.

Insights on these questions and helps for guiding a discussion using these questions are included in the Leader's Guide, which is available for download at http://www.nancyguthrie.com/even-better-than-eden.

If your group members are doing the Personal Bible Study questions for each chapter (available for download at http://www.nancyguthrie .com/even-better-than-eden), you may also want to include some or all of those questions and participant answers in your discussion.

Chapter 1: The Story of the Wilderness

1. Most of us have a sense of emptiness or discontentment at one time or another. Have you found that to be true in your life? In what ways?

2. How did the Serpent sow seeds of discontentment in Eve? How did Eve begin to see a lack in her life?

3. Perhaps you have never considered before that there was wilderness outside the garden of Eden that needed to be subdued, or that the task of Adam and Eve, along with their offspring, was to extend the boundaries of the garden until it was ordered and filled with image bearers bringing glory to God. Does all this make sense to you? Why or why not? As you consider this question in light of the purposes of God

revealed throughout the rest of the Bible, you might look at Genesis 12:3; Psalm 8; Isaiah 45:18; Acts 1:8; and Revelation 5:9–10.

4. Deuteronomy 8:3 says that God let his people hunger so that they would know that man does not live by bread alone but by every word that comes from the mouth of the Lord. What does it mean to live by every word that comes from the mouth of the Lord in our day? And how can our discontentment direct us to live this way?

5. In what way(s) did Jesus enter into the wilderness—the *tohu wabohu*—of this world, and what difference does that make?

6. What does Paul teach us about how to be content as we live in the wilderness of this world, where the thorns of the curse bring pain? (See 2 Cor. 12:1–10)

7. In what way will the garden of the new heaven and the new earth be even better than the garden Adam and Eve enjoyed in Eden?

8. How does this story of discontentment as well as contentment in the wilderness have the power to transform our own lack of contentment in the wilderness of this world?

Chapter 2: The Story of the Tree

1. How would you define "the good life"? How do you think most people in our world today define it? How do they go about getting it for themselves?

2. We aren't told if Adam and Eve ate of the tree of life before they ate of the tree of the knowledge of good and evil and were banished from Eden. What do you see in Genesis 3:22 and Revelation 2:7 that might suggest that they didn't?

3. How would you explain God's purpose for the tree of the knowledge of good and evil in Eden? For what purpose did the Serpent seek to use the tree?

4. What should Adam have done at the tree of the knowledge of good and evil?

5. How was the second Adam's response to temptation regarding the tree in stark contrast to the first Adam's, and what difference does this make for us today? Read Romans 5:12–21 together to add to your discussion.

6. In what way is the tree of life in the garden of the new heaven and the new earth even better than it was in the garden of Eden? (See Rev. 22:1–5)

7. What does the story of the tree of life from Genesis to Revelation reveal about what it means to live the good life and how to get it?

8. How does this story of the tree provide direction to us in our pursuit of the good life?

Chapter 3: The Story of His Image

1. What are the common elements of the way we often introduce ourselves to others online or in person? What do these things reveal about where we find our identity?

2. Give three or four key words that capture the essence of what it means for man to be made (and therefore renewed) in the image of God. (See Gen. 1:26; Ps. 8:5–6; Eph. 4:24; and Col. 3:10)

3. In Exodus 19:4–6 and 20:1–21 God provided his firstborn son, the nation of Israel, with a foundation for a sense of identity. What was to shape their sense of identity, and what difference should that have made in how they lived in the land God was giving to them?

4. We tend to think of idols as bad things. But often idols are good things that have become ultimate things. An idol is anything apart from Christ about which we say through our attitudes and actions, "I must have this to be happy." Most of us have no interest in bowing down

before a golden calf, but what are some idols we worship by foolishly drawing our identity from them?

5. People in the world today have lots of ideas about who Jesus is and why he came. How does this story of the image of God provide us with clarity about his identity and his purpose in coming?

6. How does considering the transfiguration and the resurrection of Jesus impact how we think about what it means to be like Jesus?

7. How will the image of God we will bear in the new creation be even better than it was for Adam and Eve in Eden?

8. How does this story of the image of God being marred and then restored have the power to change our sense of identity and destiny?

Chapter 4: The Story of Clothing

1. In Psalms 8:5 and 104:1–2 we read about how God is crowned, clothed, and covered. Since Adam and Eve were made in God's image, what do these verses suggest about how they would have been crowned, clothed, and covered even though they were physically naked?

2. Consider the significance of the clothing of royal representatives and priests throughout the Bible: Joseph in Genesis 37:3, 23 and 41:39–43; priests in Exodus 28; David in 1 Samuel 18:3–4; Daniel in Daniel 5:29; and the prodigal son in Luke 15:21–22. How might this context of the whole Bible help us to understand what Moses intends his readers to understand when he writes that Adam and Eve were naked and not ashamed?

3. We might think of someone simply as either clothed or unclothed in the glory of God, but the Bible seems to present degrees of glory. How is this made evident in 2 Corinthians 3:7–18? How might this help us understand what God intended for Adam and Eve in the garden? (See also 1 Cor. 15:40–49; 2 Cor. 5:1–5)

4. When we consider that God clothed the priests of the Old Testament in "holy garments . . . for glory and for beauty" (Ex. 28:2) along with the reality that he intends for all believers to be clothed in this way, how should it shape our perspective about public nudity and pornography?

5. The Bible's perspective on beauty is very different from the world's perspective (see Col. 3:12–14; 1 Pet. 3:4). What do you think it requires in order for our perspective about beauty to be shaped more by the Bible than by the world?

6. Paul writes in 1 Corinthians 15:52–53 and 2 Corinthians 5:1–5 about believers being clothed in immortality at the resurrection when Christ returns. How does this help us to understand Adam and Eve's nakedness in Eden and what might have been had they obeyed regarding the tree?

7. In what way will the clothing we will wear when Christ returns to bring us into the new heaven and the new earth be better than the clothing Adam and Eve had in Eden both before and after the fall?

8. In what ways does this story of clothing have the power to change how we think about the way we dress and what makes us beautiful? How does it have the power to help us with shame?

Chapter 5: The Story of the Bridegroom

1. In Genesis 2:24 how does Moses, the author of Genesis, apply the marriage of Adam and Eve to marriage in his day? What implications of this did Jesus teach in Matthew 19:3–8? What implications did Paul teach in 1 Corinthians 6:15–17?

2. In what ways was Adam and Eve's relationship impacted by sin and the curse, according to Genesis 3:6–21?

3. Where in the Scriptures would you find support for the statement, "The story of the Bible is the story of God choosing, gathering, and beautifying a bride for his Son"? (Think through all parts of both Old and New Testaments to find either general or specific scriptural support.)

4. How should the Israelites in their day have understood John the Baptist's description of Jesus as the Bridegroom and Jesus's own depiction of himself in parables as the Bridegroom? What would it have meant for them if they had understood and embraced that reality?

5. How does seeing the story of the woman at the well through the lens of the Bible's bridegroom imagery help us to grasp both the nature of Christ's bride and the nature of Jesus as a bridegroom? (See John 4)

6. What are the implications of Paul's statement in Ephesians 5:31–32? How do these verses help us to understand Genesis 2 and Revelation 21?

7. In what ways will the marriage we will enjoy in the new heaven and the new earth be even better than the marriage of Adam and Eve in Eden?

8. In what ways does this story of the bridegroom have the power to change our expectations regarding human marriage as well as our anticipation of the ultimate marriage?

Chapter 6: The Story of Sabbath

1. What has been your understanding of the Sabbath or the Lord's Day in the past? Have you seen it as a gift or as a burden? Would you say you have leaned more toward legalism or neglect?

2. Genesis 2 doesn't say explicitly that Adam and Eve were to rest from their work every seventh day. But how might the pattern in Genesis 1 and 2 of Adam and Eve imitating God in his work of bringing order to the creation, lead us to that conclusion?

3. How would you explain the purpose of God's command to Israel that not only their weeks but also their years, the use of their land, and the collection of debt would take a sabbath shape?

4. Like so many of God's commands for the good of his people, the Sabbath command became twisted and burdensome over time. How was the Sabbath ignored in the Old Testament era and separated from true godliness by the time Jesus came?

5. What do you sense from the Gospels was Jesus's message regarding the Sabbath? (See Matt. 12:1–14; Mark 2:23–28)

6. There is no New Testament command to keep the Sabbath. However, there are some strong biblical arguments to suggest that God still intends his people to receive the gift of a weekly sabbath to nurture their longing for rest with him. None of the other Ten Commandments, which were written on stone, have been rescinded. Hebrews 4:9 says that "there remains a Sabbath rest remains for the people of God," which we have not yet entered into and still need to be regularly reoriented toward. How does considering the Sabbath in light of the overarching Bible story shape your understanding of what God intends for believers in this age?

7. How will the sabbath rest we will enjoy in the new heaven and the new earth be even better than Adam and Eve would have enjoyed in Eden?

8. How might this story of sabbath change the way you approach the Lord's Day?

Chapter 7: The Story of Offspring

1. At the heart of the story of the offspring of the woman and the offspring of the Serpent is enmity or conflict. How is this enmity both divine judgment and divine grace?

2. How does understanding the story of the offspring help us to make sense of:

    • the numerous genealogies in the Old and New Testaments

    • the dominance of battle between Israel and her enemies in the narratives of the Old Testament

    • the imprecatory psalms such as Psalms 69 and 109

    • the prominence of demonic activity in the Gospels

    • the importance of Jesus being born of a woman

    • the need for spiritual armor to engage in spiritual warfare

3. How does this story of the offspring add to your understanding of what happened in the crucifixion of Jesus?

4. How does this story add to your understanding of what it means to have peace with God?

5. How does this story shape your understanding of what it means to be protected by God, and how you should pray about protection from God?

6. What does this story of the offspring reveal about how the new heaven and the new earth will be even better than Eden?

7. How does the story of the offspring help you to make sense of some of the struggles you have faced in your life, and how does it provide hope and confidence for your future?

Chapter 8: The Story of a Dwelling Place

1. In Genesis 1 and 2 we read about God's creation of a home that he can share with humanity made in his image. How does understanding God's intention to dwell with a holy people in a holy land help us to make sense of the rest of the Bible's story?

2. Many chapters in Exodus are dedicated to the design and building of the tabernacle, and many chapters in 1 Kings and 1 Chronicles are dedicated to the design and building of the temple. Many psalms speak of God's dwelling place or house. And the Prophetic Books have much to say about the defilement of the temple, the destruction of the temple, and the rebuilding of the temple. Why do you think so much attention is given in the Old Testament to this tent and building?

3. Though God came down to dwell among his people in the Most Holy Place of the tabernacle and later the temple, there was still a problem. What was it? And how was this problem eventually dealt with?

4. How would you describe Jesus's relationship to the temple in Jerusalem as recorded throughout the Gospels?

5. What is your understanding of God's dwelling place in this age between Christ's ascension and return?

6. Do you think a longing to be relieved of living in this sin-sick world is the same thing as a longing to be at home with God? Why or why not? What kinds of things keep us from longing to be at home with God?

7. In what ways will our eternal home with God be even better than Eden?

8. How does this story of God's intention to dwell with his people have the power to change how you live your life as a walking, talking temple of the Holy Spirit?

Chapter 9: The Story of the City

1. What are some things the cities of Enoch, Sodom, Babel, and Babylon had in common?

2. What did the cities of Sodom and Nineveh have in common, and what was different about them? (See Gen. 10:10–12; 13:12–13, 19; Jonah 3:1–10)

3. Jerusalem was the city where God himself made his home in the temple. It is the city where God's king reigned. It was full of potential. But what happened to the city of Jerusalem and why?

4. What do the stories of Lot in Sodom and God's people exiled in Babylon reveal about the tension of being in the world but not of the world?

5. If the command to God's people in Revelation is to "come out" of Babylon lest we take part in her sins, what should that look like?

6. In what ways do we both take comfort and feel sorrow in the Bible's portrayal of Babylon's destiny?

7. How will life in the New Jerusalem be even better than life in Eden?

8. How does this story of the city change how we live now in the city of man? In what ways do we live and operate differently in this city as citizens of heaven from those who are citizens of the city of man?

Notes

Introduction

1. "It is not biblical to hold that eschatology is a sort of appendix to soteriology, a consummation of the saving work of God. . . . There is an absolute end posited for the universe before and apart from sin. The universe, as created, was only a beginning, the meaning of which was not perpetuation, but attainment. The principle of God's relation to the world from the outset was a principle of action or eventuation. The goal was not comparative (i.e., evolution); it was superlative (i.e., the final goal). This goal was not only previous to sin, but irrespective of sin." Geerhardus Vos, *The Eschatology of the Old Testament* (Phillipsburg, NJ: P&R, 2001), 73.

Chapter 1: The Story of the Wilderness

1. "The Wind of God began to move upon the face of the waters. The Wind here broods like a hen over an unhatched cosmos, waiting to see what this unformed universe will hatch." Calvin Miller, *Loving God Up Close* (Nashville, TN: Warner Faith, 2004), 10.

2. "There was a difference between the conditions inside and outside the garden. Genesis 2:5 states that 'no bush of the field was yet in the land,' a reference to field vegetation fit only for animal grazing. On the other hand 'no small plant of the field had yet sprung up,' a reference to agriculture grown with irrigation and human effort for consumption as food. This division between field vegetation and cultivated agriculture means that there was a noticeable boundary between the garden and the outside world. God sent rain and created man to grow food (Gen. 2:6–7), and therefore in the immediate area of the garden there was order." J. V. Fesko, *Last Things First: Unlocking Genesis 1–3 with the Christ of Eschatology* (Ross-shire, UK: Christian Focus, 2007), 98.

3. "The aim of spreading God's glory worldwide through glorious image-bearers is to be understood more specifically as extending the boundaries of the Eden temple (which continued the divine glory) around the entire earth." Greg Beale, *A New Testament Biblical Theology: The Unfolding of the Old Testament in the New* (Grand Rapids, MI: Baker Academic, 2011), 38. Later he writes, "The intention seems to be that Adam was to widen

the boundaries of the garden in ever-increasing circles by extending the order of the garden sanctuary into the inhospitable outer spaces. The outward expansion would include the goal of spreading the glorious presence of God. This would be accomplished especially by Adam's progeny born in his image and thus reflecting God's image and the light of his presence, as they continued to obey the mandate given to their parents and went out to subdue the outer country until the Eden sanctuary covered the earth." Ibid., 622.

4. "The covenant of works, instituted in the Garden of Eden, was the promise that perfect obedience would be rewarded with eternal life. Adam was created sinless but with the capability of falling into sin. Had he remained faithful in the time of temptation in the Garden (the 'probationary period'), he would have been made incapable of sinning and secured in an eternal and unbreakable right standing with God." Matt Perman, "What Does John Piper Believe about Dispensationalism, Covenant Theology, and New Covenant Theology?" Desiring God website, January 23, 2011, accessed May 1, 2017, http://www.desiringgod.org/articles/what-does-john-piper-believe-about-dispensationalism-covenant-theology-and-new-covenant-theology.

5. William Williams, "Guide Me, O Thou Great Jehovah," 1745.

Chapter 2: The Story of the Tree

1. *Broadcast News*, directed by James L. Brooks (Culver City, CA: Gracie Films, 1987).

2. "Although the Scripture does not make express mention of a heavenly life to be conferred on Adam it is with sufficient clearness gathered by legitimate consequence from the opposed threatening of eternal death and from the sacramental seal of this promise by the tree of life (the signification of which was surely known to man). For although Moses describes is obscurely (as most of the things pertaining to that covenant, upon which, as the shadow of a fleeing image, he throws only scattered rays of light to represent its evanescence), yet there can be no doubt that these things were more distinctly revealed to the first man." Francis Turretin, *Institutes of Elenctic Theology*, ed. James T. Dennison Jr., trans. George M. Giger, 3 vols. (Phillipsburg, NJ: P&R, 1997), 1:585.

3. The Westminster Confession (7.2) reads, "The first covenant made with man was a covenant of works, wherein life was promised to Adam, and in him to his posterity, upon condition of perfect and personal obedience." See Gen. 2:17; Rom. 5:12–20; 10:5; Gal. 3:10–12.

4. Augustine, *The Literal Meaning of Genesis*, vol. 2, Ancient Christian Writers, trans. John Hammond Taylor (Mahwah, NJ: Paulist Press, 1982), 38.

5. Turretin, *Institutes of Elenctic Theology*, 1:581.

6. In *Notes on Scripture* (*Works of Jonathan Edwards*, ed. Stephen J. Stein [New Haven, CT: Yale University Press, 1998], 15:392–96), Jonathan Edwards suggests that the tree of life did not bear fruit until the proba-

tionary period was past. Meredith Kline suggests that the word "also" in Genesis 3:22 ("Now, lest he reach out his hand and take *also* of the tree of life and eat, and live forever") implies that "partaking of the tree of life was reserved for an appropriate future time and purpose." Meredith Kline, *Kingdom Prologue: Genesis Foundations for a Covenantal Worldview* (Eugene, OR: Wipf & Stock), 94.

7. Some theologians believe that Adam and Eve had been eating from this tree all along since God had said, "You may surely eat of every tree of the garden" (Gen. 2:16). However one aspect of the life provided by eating of the tree of life is being impervious to sin and death, and that was certainly not the case for Adam and Eve. Another support for the proposition that Adam and Eve did not eat of the tree of life prior to the fall is found in Rev. 2:7, which speaks of eating of the tree of life being granted to those who "overcome" or "conquer," meaning those who overcome the temptations of this world. Clearly, Adam and Eve did not overcome the world and its temptations, which would suggest it had not yet been granted to them to eat of this tree.

8. Thomas Boston, *The Whole Works of the Late Reverend Thomas Boston of Ettrick*, vol. 11 (Aberdeen, UK: George and Robert King, 1852), 193.

9. Francis Turretin offers five reasons that God placed the tree of the knowledge of good and evil in Eden. See Turretin, *Institutes of Elenctic Theology*, 1:579–80.

10. "The tree in Eden seems to have been the symbolic place where judgment was to be carried out (much as courthouses and courtrooms are adorned with the symbol of Lady Justice). The name of the tree—'the tree of the knowledge of good and evil'—of which Adam was not to eat, was suggestive of his magisterial duty. 'Discerning between good and evil' is a Hebrew expression that refers to kings or authoritative figures being able to make judgments in carrying out justice." Greg Beale, *A New Testament Biblical Theology: The Unfolding of the Old Testament in the New* (Grand Rapids, MI: Baker Academic, 2011), 35.

11. "Spiritually our first parents became dead in the day they sinned. Their sin constituted this death; they estranged themselves from God and their mind became enmity against God. Judicially they also died in the day they sinned; they became subject to the curse. Psycho-physical death can be said to have befallen them the day they sinned, in that mortality became their lot." John Murray, *Collected Writings*, 4 vols. (Edinburgh: Banner of Truth, 1977), 2:56.

12. "This is the truth and mystery shadowed in this ancient type: the tree of life—not earthly, but heavenly; not material and irrational (*alogos*), but mystical and rational; not only significative and sealing of life, but truly the bestower of it. 'In him was life' (Jn. 1:4, i.e., the fountain and cause of all life). . . . Truly he is the only tree because no one except Christ is the author of eternal life (nor is there salvation in any other, Acts 4:12). No one except Christ is in the midst of paradise (Rev. 2:7) and of the street of

the city (Rev. 22:2). Christ is in the midst of the church (as a more honorable and suitable place) to be near all and diffuse his vivifying power among all; to be seen by all, as the center in which all the lines of faith and love ought to meet, that they may acquiesce in him. The fruit-bearing tree (Rev. 2:7), which bears the sweetest and most exquisite fruit for the support of believers (Cant. 2:3), bears twelve kinds of them (Rev. 22:2), i.e., the most abundant and richest, sufficing for the twelve tribes of Israel (i.e., for all the members of the church, which from his fullness draw all gifts necessary for them). It bears them every month (i.e., perpetually) because the power and efficacy of the righteousness and spirit of Christ are perpetual and unceasing for the consolation and sanctification of believers. Its leaves (never falling and perpetually green) are appointed for the healing of the nations because it has the virtue not only of aliment (to feed our souls), but also of medicine (most healthful to cure all our diseases, Is. 53:5; Mt. 11:28)." Turretin, *Institutes of Elenctic Theology*, 1:582.

13. George Bennard, "The Old Rugged Cross," 1913.

Chapter 3: The Story of His Image

1. These humorous Twitter bios created by Mark Shaefer are featured in various blog posts at https://www.businessesgrow.com. Quoted by permission.

2. Gen. 2:25 does state that Adam and Eve were naked before they sinned. More about what that means will be addressed in the next chapter.

3. See Anthony A. Hoekema, *Created in God's Image* (Grand Rapids, MI: Eerdmans, 1986), 68–73.

4. "What people revere, they resemble, either for ruin or restoration." G. K. Beale, *We Become What We Worship: A Biblical Theology of Idolatry* (Downers Grove, IL: InterVarsity, 2008), 16.

5. Greg Beale, *A New Testament Biblical Theology: The Unfolding of the Old Testament in the New* (Grand Rapids, MI: Baker Academic, 2011), 367.

6. Christopher J. H. Wright, *Knowing Jesus Through the Old Testament* (Downers Grove, IL: InterVarsity Press, 1992), ix.

7. See Hoekema, *Created in God's Image*, 91.

8. See Phil. 3:20; Eph. 2:19; Col. 3:1–4; 1 Pet. 2:9.

9. "We do not mean to say that our final state is Eden restored *simplicitier* [simply restored]. Rather, Eden is transcended: the glory with which Adam was vested in Eden is restored in those in Christ, but the final consummation of this glory will result in a state superior even to that of Eden, for there will be no possibility of reversion or fall. We will then enjoy the final state of perfected beatitude in communion with God that Adam and Eve would have enjoyed had they continued acting in trusting obedience." Dane Ortlund, "Inaugurated Glorification: Revisiting Romans 8:30," *Journal of the Evangelical Theological Society* 57 (2014): 116.

10. Rev. 2:17; 3:12.

11. "Heaven will not be a static experience. It will not flow out as one un-differentiated blur, not endless sameness, but variation and succession and newness. Heaven will unfold before us in ages, in one new era after another. . . . He will bring ever greater honor to himself as we gasp in joyful wonder over new and startling displays of his glory and holiness and righteousness and love and justice and mercy and truth and wisdom and creativity and vastness and power." Raymond Ortlund Jr., sermon, August 7, 2005, Christ Presbyterian Church, Nashville, TN.

12. Adelaide A. Pollard, "Have Thine Own Way, Lord," 1906.

Chapter 4: The Story of Clothing

1. G. William Domhoff, *Finding Meaning in Dreams: A Quantitative Approach* (New York: Plenum Press, 1996), 204. The study quoted by Domhoff states that three-fourths of the men and over half of the women they sampled report having a dream in which they were flying under their own power. They found that 40 to 50 percent of both males and females report having dreams in which they were undressed or inappropriately dressed in public accompanied by a strong emotional feeling of extreme embarrassment.

2. "Some early Jewish and Christian writings express the belief that Adam and Eve were clothed in glorious garments before the fall, lost that glory, and then wrongly tried to cover their inglorious shame with fig leaves. Some also held that the new set of clothes given to Adam and Eve in Genesis 3:21 actually possessed some degree of glory or designated Adam the first high priest or pointed to a greater inheritance of the final glorious clothing of immortality." Greg Beale, *A New Testament Biblical Theology: The Unfolding of the Old Testament in the New* (Grand Rapids, MI: Baker Academic, 2011), 453.

3. "Modern interpreters have so focused on the shame-covering function of clothing that they generally miss what ancient interpreters took for granted: the use of clothing as a means of beauty, glory, even royal majesty. . . . In the ancient Near East, kings and idols alike insofar as they represented the gods—were expected to be clothed as a sign and mark of their royal authority. It is true that the unashamed nakedness of Adam and Eve in Gen 2:25 cannot itself be seen as an investiture (clothing) with God's glory, as most ancient interpreters believed. On the other hand, it is important not to neglect the way in which nakedness without shame (Gen 2:25) still points to the need for clothing—if not as an antidote to shame, then as a means to royal honor." William N. Wilder, "Illumination and Investiture: The Royal Significance of the Tree of Wisdom in Genesis 3," *Westminster Theological Journal* 68 (2006): 58, 62.

4. See Gen. 37:3, 23; 41:39–43; 1 Sam. 18:3–4; Dan. 5:29; Luke 15:21–22.

5. "By virtue of his creation in the image of God, man under the original covenant had the status of ruler of the earth under God, a glory that reflected the dominion exercised in the heavenly court by God and the angelic hosts. As image of God, man also possessed the ethical glory of

a state of simple righteousness, with the prospect of moving on to the greater glory of confirmed righteousness." Meredith Kline, *Kingdom Prologue: Genesis Foundations for a Covenantal Worldview* (Eugene, OR: Wipf & Stock, 2006), 44–45.

6. I was helped to understand this through a podcasted conversation between Will Wood, Camden Bucey, and Jared Oliphint: "Ephesians 6:10–17 and a Biblical Theology of Clothing," Christ the Center podcast, Reformed Forum website, April 1, 2016.

7. "It would appear that the skin coverings, as the antithetical counterpart of the image of the devil, are to be understood as symbols of adornment with the glory of the image of God. (Compare the later use of animal skins among the tabernacle coverings that were symbolic replicas of the divine Glory.)" Meredith Kline, *Images of the Spirit* (Eugene, OR: Wipf & Stock, 1999), 150.

8. This description of the priests' clothing is adapted from my earlier book *The Lamb of God: Seeing Jesus in Exodus, Leviticus, Numbers, and Deuteronomy*, Seeing Jesus in the Old Testament (Wheaton, IL: Crossway), 2012, 174–75.

9. "Paul is exhorting them to stop being identified with the traits of the former life in the first Adam and to be characterized by those of the new life in the last Adam." Beale, *New Testament Biblical Theology*, 842.

10. "We may interpret the nakedness spoken of here as meaning the lack of the full glory of this heavenly type of existence. In this sense even our present earthly life is characterized by nakedness, in distinction from our being clothed upon with heavenly glory." Anthony A. Hoekema, *The Bible and the Future* (Grand Rapids, MI: Eerdmans, 1979), 106–7.

11. "If Adam is dishonorable, it can be understood not ethically, but eschatologically. Adam is dishonorable in the sense that he has not yet been glorified. He is dishonorable, not in the sense that he has sinned, but that he hasn't reached the highest honor as a creature. He has not yet been glorified. The contrast is between dishonor and honor, or glory." Lane Tipton, "The Covenant of Works, Adam's Destiny," lecture in ST131: Survey of Reformed Theology (2014), Westminster Theological Seminary, Glenside, PA, accessed March 25, 2015, via ITunesU.

12. Forgive me, dear reader, if it seems as if I've brushed past something significant in my desire to keep the main thing of this chapter the main thing. If you are unfamiliar with the story of the brief lives of our daughter, Hope, and later our son Gabriel, you can find more at www.nancyguthrie .com, or in my books *Holding on to Hope* (Carol Stream, IL: Tyndale, 2002) and *Hearing Jesus Speak Into Your Sorrow* (Carol Stream, IL: Tyndale, 2009).

13. Augustus Toplady, "Rock of Ages, Cleft for Me," 1776.

Chapter 5: The Story of the Bridegroom

1. If you enjoyed that poem, you might also enjoy this poem David wrote to me after I shrunk one of his favorite sweaters in the wash: To Nancy,

My Sweater-heart, February 12, 2011: Our love is like a sweater, / All fuzzy, warm and soft, / And I'm not talkin' Wal-Mart, here. / But more Ann Taylor Loft. / For those intent on showing off, / Wear dresses, suits, or better, / But we who favor comfort know, / You just can't beat a sweater! / I'm a pushover for your pullover, / You're a major fan to my cardigan, / I'd throw a fit for your cable knit / You're crazy as heck for my turtleneck. / When the moths of hardship nibble at / the fabric of our life, / Our hearts, now knit together know, / We're more than man and wife / See, our love is like a sweater, / The most beautiful, I think, / And even in hot water, / Impossible to shrink!

2. "It is not good, not because he is lonely (he may or may not be!), but quite simply because the job is too big for him to do on his own. This is why he is given 'a helper' rather than 'a companion.' . . . She is given to him here as his 'helper,' which simply means one who works alongside so that both together can do the task." Christopher Ash, *Married for God: Making Your Marriage the Best It Can Be* (Wheaton, IL: Crossway, 2016), 36.

3. R. Kent Hughes, *Genesis: Beginning and Blessing*, Preaching the Word, ed. R. Kent Hughes (Wheaton, IL: Crossway, 2004), 58.

4. This insight comes from William Taylor, "God's Purpose in Marriage," sermon, January 30, 2001, St. Helens Bishopsgate, London.

5. See Ex. 18:4; Deut. 33:7; 1 Sam. 7:12; Pss. 20; 121:1–2; 124:8.

6. Ray Ortlund Jr., *Marriage and the Mystery of the Gospel*, Short Studies in Biblical Theology (Wheaton, IL: Crossway, 2016), 30.

7. I found Nick Batzig's summary of views on possible interpretations of this verse helpful: http://www.reformation21.org/blog/2016/09/desiring-to-rule-over-genesis.php.

8. "Given Paul's interpretation of Genesis 2:24, this logically requires that Eve is a type of the Church. . . . Christ has taken up the work of the dominion mandate and with the assistance of his helpmate, his bride, the second Eve, the Church, is now fulfilling it." J. V. Fesko, *Last Things First: Unlocking Genesis 1–3 with the Christ of Eschatology* (Ross-shire, UK: Christian Focus, 2007), 167–75.

9. John Piper, *This Momentary Marriage: A Parable of Permanence* (Wheaton, IL: Crossway, 2009), 128.

10. S. J. Stone, "The Church's One Foundation," 1866.

Chapter 6: The Story of Sabbath

1. Chad Bird, "The Missing Verse in the Creation Account," http://www.chadbird.com/blog/2015/08/28/the-missing-verse-in-the-creation-account.

2. "God's own work of six days and a seventh day of rest indicates that Adam was to emulate this pattern in his own work. How long this work would have taken is unknown." J. V. Fesko, *Last Things First: Unlocking Genesis 1–3 with the Christ of Eschatology* (Ross-shire, UK: Christian Focus, 2007), 102.

3. This rest of consummation was introduced into the life of man in order to show him his goal. Even in unfallen man the Sabbath was an

eschatological sign because its meaning lies in the relation of man and God. It is important to note this because it bears witness to the fundamental element of eschatology in religion. Eschatology is the essence of true religion as it is shown by its pre-redemptive existence." Geerhardus Vos, *The Eschatology of the Old Testament* (Phillipsburg, NJ: P&R, 2001), 75.

4. "The exact relationship between the tree of life, Adam's work, and the eschatological rest of the seventh day is unknown. One may surmise that Adam would have performed the labors of the covenant of works and with each passing Sabbath rested from his labors in anticipation of the completion of his work and entrance into the eternal seventh day rest of God." Ibid., 184. Also: "Although Adam is not explicitly said to imitate God in resting on the seventh day of each week, many have discerned in Gen. 2:3 a creational mandate for humanity to rest on the seventh day of each week. . . . Would not Adam, created in the image of God, be expected to reflect God's goal of resting at the end of the creative process, since clearly he is to reflect the first two creative activities leading to that goal?" Greg Beale, *A New Testament Biblical Theology: The Unfolding of the Old Testament in the New* (Grand Rapids, MI: Baker Academic, 2011), 776–77.

5. "Adam had the responsibility of fulfilling his covenantal obligations, after which he would have entered into a permanent Sabbath rest. The probation would have ended, death would no longer have been a possibility, *posse non mori*, and Adam would have rested from his duties as vicegerent over the creation once the earth was filled with the image and glory of God." Fesko, *Last Things First*, 103. Also: "Had its probation been successful, then the sacramental Sabbath would have passed over into the reality it typified, and the entire subsequent course of the history of the race would have been radically different." Geerhardus Vos, *Biblical Theology* (Eugene, OR: Wipf & Stock, 2003), 140.

6. "The work which issues into the rest can now no longer be man's own work. It becomes the work of Christ." Vos, *Biblical Theology*, 141.

7. "Israel was supposed to dwell in this garden-like land, worship and serve God, multiply the image of God and worship of him throughout the earth, and upon the completion of their work enter the eternal Sabbath rest of God." Fesko, *Last Things First*, 127–28.

8. Bird, "The Missing Verse in the Creation Account."

9. See Matt. 28:1; Mark 16:2; Luke 24:1; John 20:1.

10. See 1 Cor. 4:14; 7:8; Gal. 4:19; 1 Tim. 1:2; 2 Tim. 1:2; Philem. 10; Titus 1:4.

11. A highly credible view that draws a different conclusion than what I'm suggesting in this chapter can be found at https://blogs.thegospelcoalition.org/justintaylor/2010/10/14/schreiner-qa-is-the-sabbath-still-required-for-christians/ or in the book the article is drawn from: Thomas Schreiner, *40 Questions about Christians and Biblical Law*, 40 Questions and Answers, ed. Benjamin Merkle (Grand Rapids, MI: Kregel, 2010), 209–18. Another credible book that argues an alternate view is *From Sabbath to Lord's Day: A Biblical, Historical and Theological Investigation*, ed. D. A. Carson (Eugene, OR: Wipf & Stock,

1999). In support of the view presented here is Richard Gaffin's chapter, "A Sabbath Rest Still Awaits the People of God," in *Pressing Toward the Mark*, ed. Charles G. Dennison and Richard C. Gamble (Philadelphia: Committee for the Historian of the Orthodox Presbyterian Church, 1986).

12. "Part of the function of Mosaic law in the history of redemption was to act as a temporary *paedagogos*, a schoolmaster or tutor teaching God's old covenant people of their need for a Savior (Gal. 3:24–25). Thus, the Sabbath remained on Saturday, at the end of our weekly labors, a kind of enacted promise, offering Israel eternal rest should she perfectly obey the law. The persistence of the Sabbath, at the end of a week of imperfect obedience, was intended to teach Israel to look for a second Adam who would accomplish the ultimate exodus-redemption and obtain for His people the final Sabbath rest that the first Adam forfeited and our best works cannot now hope to secure. . . . Now that 'it is finished' (John 19:30), the Sabbath day comes no longer at the end of a week of work but at the beginning of it. The work by which the Sabbath rest is secured has been accomplished for us by Jesus. Now we rest in Him and work in the strength His saving grace supplies (Heb. 3:7–4:10). . . . That's why the church now meets on the first day of the week (John 20:19; Acts 20:7; 1 Cor. 16:2; Rev. 1:10). New creation and perfect redemption are the great realities that are ours already in Christ, and we celebrate them and enjoy them on the Christian Sabbath day. It is a gospel ordinance that is refreshing for us and glorifying to God." David Strain, "A Well-Spent Sabbath," *Tabletalk* magazine, February, 2015, http://www.ligonier.org/learn/articles/well-spent-sabbath.

13. "The shift of the weekly Sabbath from the seventh day to the first day reflects the present eschatological situation of the church—the change to the first day is an index of eschatology already realized, of the eschatological new-creation rest inaugurated by Christ, especially by his resurrection; the continuation of a weekly rest-day is a sign of eschatology still future, a pointer to the eschatological rest to come at Christ's return." Gaffin, "A Sabbath Rest Still Awaits the People of God," in *Pressing toward the Mark*, 51n37.

14. The Westminster Confession of Faith (21.8) reads, "This Sabbath is to be kept holy unto the Lord when men, after a due preparing of their hearts, and ordering of their common affairs beforehand, do not only observe an holy rest all the day from their own works, words, and thoughts about their worldly employments and recreations, but also are taken up the whole time in the public and private exercises of His worship, and in the duties of necessity and mercy."

15. Charles Wesley, "Love Divine, All Loves Excelling," 1757.

Chapter 7: The Story of Offspring

1. This characterization of God's intended message to Adam and Eve is adapted from Ligon Duncan, "An Ancient Christmas: The Coming of the

Christ in the Old Testament—The Seed," sermon, December 2, 2012, First Presbyterian Church, Jackson, Mississippi.

2. Geerhardus Vos, *Biblical Theology* (Eugene, OR: Wipf & Stock, 2003), 42.

3. This is made explicit in 1 John 3:12, where John writes that Cain "was of the evil one and murdered his brother."

4. "In Egypt, such a pole or standard was a recognized symbol of the deity's power. Here it served to demonstrate that the Lord's power was present in the midst of the camp, granting life to those whose sins had condemned them to death through the serpent's bite. The transfixed serpent on the standard thus demonstrated in visual terms the defeat of Israel's mortal enemies, Egypt and Satan, overcome by the power of the Lord. . . . The people were to look intently at the bronze serpent, putting their trust in the power of the Lord's victory over evil, and then they would be healed." Iain Duguid, *Numbers: God's Presence in the Wilderness,* Preaching the Word, ed. R. Kent Hughes (Wheaton, IL: Crossway, 2006), 263. While the text does not indicate that the head of the serpent on the pole was crushed, it makes sense that the way in which it was attached to the pole would have pictured the means of their salvation, the crushing of the Serpent's head.

5. A more complete treatment of my pursuit to understand God's promises of protection throughout the Scriptures can be found in my book *Hearing Jesus Speak into Your Sorrow* (Carol Stream, IL: Tyndale, 2009).

6. Martin Luther, "A Mighty Fortress Is Our God," 1529.

Chapter 8: The Story of a Dwelling Place

1. My husband, David, along with his business partner, Rob Howard, creates fabulous, funny, scripturally sound kids' musicals for churches and Christian schools through their company, Little Big Stuff Music, which is based in our home. See https://littlebigstuff.com/.

2. "The garden is 'the garden of God,' not in the first instance an abode for man as such, but specifically a place of reception of man into fellowship with God in God's own dwelling-place. . . . There can be no doubt concerning the principle of paradise being the habitation of God, where He dwells in order to make man dwell with Himself." Geerhardus Vos, *Biblical Theology* (Eugene, OR: Wipf & Stock, 2003), 27–28.

3. "The key phrase describing God's approach through the garden, traditionally translated 'in the cool of the day,' should be rendered 'as the Spirit of the day.' 'Spirit' here denotes the theophanic Glory, as it does in Genesis 1:2 and elsewhere in Scripture. And 'the day' has the connotation it often has in the prophets' forecasts of the great coming judgment (cf. also Judg. 11:27 and 1 Cor. 4:3). Here in Genesis 3:8 is the original day of the Lord, which served as the prototypal mold in which subsequent pictures of other days of the Lord were cast." Meredith Kline, *Kingdom Prologue: Genesis Foundations for a Covenantal Worldview* (Eugene, OR: Wipf & Stock, 2006), 129.

4. See G. K. Beale and Mitchell Kim, *God Dwells Among Us* (Downers Grove, IL: InterVarsity Press, 2014), 21–23.
5. See Nancy Guthrie, *The Word of the Lord: Seeing Jesus in the Prophets* (Wheaton, IL: Crossway, 2014), 223.
6. See ibid., 226–29.
7. When the veil of the temple split from top to bottom, it put an end to the three divisions of the tabernacle/temple. The Spirit dwells in believers now so that we have become the "holy place" where God dwells. When we read in Revelation 22 about the dimensions of the new city/garden, it is a perfect cube, suggesting that the whole earth will have become the Most Holy Place. The promise of Rev. 22:4, that the inhabitants of the garden-city-temple will "see his face," indicates that all will have open access to God and the Lamb.
8. Isaac Watts, "O God, Our Help in Ages Past," 1719.

Chapter 9: The Story of the City

1. "These are the 20 Greatest Cities to Live In," Telegraph Media Group Ltd., June 14, 2017, http://www.telegraph.co.uk/travel/galleries/The-worlds-most-liveable-cities/.
2. When David took the city of Jerusalem, it came to be known as the "city of David," or "Zion." David brought the ark of the covenant to the stronghold of Zion so that it became the center of worship and God's presence. When we hear Jerusalem referred to as "Zion" throughout the Old Testament, it is indicating the city of God's presence, the center of the hopes of God's people, the source of help to God's people. The prophets and the psalmists continually speak of Zion as the place from which the Lord will one day rule over the nations as King, so there is a future orientation to Zion as well as a past orientation. But there is also a present aspect to Zion. The writer of Hebrews says of those who have trusted in Christ, "You have come to Mount Zion and to the city of the living God, the heavenly Jerusalem" (Heb. 12:22). To be in Christ is to have permanent citizenship in Zion, the city of God.
3. Jacques Ellul, *The Meaning of the City* (Grand Rapids, MI: Eerdmans, 1970), 139–40.
4. "The book of Revelation clearly retains significance for the historical city of Jerusalem in the eschatological understanding of the early church. . . . John's depiction of the final revolt against 'the city he loves' after the thousand-year reign clearly places the future city of Jerusalem in the center of the eschatological picture. . . . A future for Jerusalem thus comports well with a future millennial reign of Christ in which Israel as a nation plays a central role." Robert L. Saucy, *The Case for Progressive Dispensationalism* (Grand Rapids, MI: Zondervan, 1993), 295–96.
5. G. K. Beale repeatedly describes the new heaven and the new earth as a "garden-like city in the shape of a temple," in *The Temple and the Church's Mission: A Biblical Theology of the Dwelling Place of God* (Downers Grove, IL: InterVarsity Press, 2004).

6. I wonder if Jesus was thinking of Psalm 87 when he said to Nicodemus, a proud citizen of the earthly Jerusalem, "Truly, truly, I say to you, unless one is born again he cannot see the kingdom of God" (John 3:3).

7. Isaac Watts, "We're Marching to Zion," 1707.

Bibliography

Alexander, T. Desmond. *From Eden to the New Jerusalem: An Introduction to Biblical Theology*. Grand Rapids, MI: Kregel Academic & Professional, 2009.

Ash, Christopher. *Married for God: Making Your Marriage the Best It Can Be*. Wheaton, IL: Crossway, 2016.

Batzig, Nick. "A Biblical Theology of Clothing." *The Christward Collective* (blog), March 3, 2015. Accessed November 7, 2016. http://info.alliance net.org/christward/a-biblical-theology-of-clothing.

———. "Jesus, the True and Greater Gardener." *The Christward Collective* (blog), September 25, 2014. Accessed November 7, 2016. http://info .alliancenet.org/christward/jesus-the-true-and-greater-gardener.

———. "The Sin-Bearing, Curse-Removing Second Adam." *The Christward Collective* (blog), August 5, 2014. Accessed November 7, 2016. http:// www.christwardcollective.com/christward/the-sin-bearing-curse -removing-second-adam-part-1.

———. "A Tale of Two Trees." *The Christward Collective* (blog), May 13, 2014. Accessed March 29, 2017. http://www.christwardcollective.com /christward/a-tale-of-two-trees.

Beale, G. K. *A New Testament Biblical Theology: The Unfolding of the Old Testament in the New*. Grand Rapids, MI: Baker Academic, 2012.

———. *Revelation: A Shorter Commentary*. Grand Rapids, MI: Eerdmans, 2015.

Beale, G. K., and Mitchell Kim. *God Dwells among Us: Expanding Eden to the Ends of the Earth*. Nottingham, UK: Inter-Varsity Press, 2015.

Begg, Alistair. "Holy Day or Holiday." Sermon, Parkside Church, Chagrin Falls, OH, October 3, 1993. Accessed April 8, 2017. https://www.truth forlife.org/resources/sermon/holy-day-or-holiday-pt1/.

Begg, Alistair, and Sinclair B. Ferguson. *Name Above All Names*. Wheaton, IL: Crossway, 2013.

Bird, Chad. "The Missing Verse in the Creation Account." *Chad Bird* (blog), August 28, 2015. Accessed May 21, 2017. http://www.chadbird.com /blog/2015/08/28/the-missing-verse-in-the-creation-account.

Bucey, Camden. "Eschatology and the Image of the Last Adam." Lecture, 2016 Reformed Forum Theology Conference, Hope Orthodox Presbyterian Church, Grayslake, IL, October 26, 2016. Accessed May 18, 2017. http://reformedforum.org/category/series/events /2016-theology-conference/.

Clowney, Edmund P. *The Unfolding Mystery: Discovering Christ in the Old Testament: with Study and Application Questions*. Phillipsburg, NJ: P&R, 2013.

Clowney, Edmund Prosper, and Rebecca Clowney Jones. *How Jesus Transforms the Ten Commandments*. Phillipsburg, NJ: P&R, 2007.

Duncan, Ligon. "An Ancient Christmas: The Coming of Jesus in the Old Testament (The Seed)." Sermon, First Presbyterian Church, Jackson, MS, December 2, 2012. Accessed June 19, 2017. http://www.fpcjackson .org/resource-library/sermons/the-seed-of-the-woman.

———. "Covenant of Works." Lecture, Reformed Theological Seminary, Jackson, MS, October 4, 2013. Accessed May 11, 2017. http://ligonduncan .com/covenant-of-works-creation-1199/.

Ellul, Jacques, and Dennis Pardee. *The Meaning of the City*. Eugene, OR: Wipf & Stock, 2011.

Fesko, J. V. *Last Things First: Unlocking Genesis 1–3 with the Christ of Eschatology*. Fearn, Ross-shire, UK: Mentor, 2007.

Gaffin, Richard. "A Sabbath Rest Still Awaits the People of God." In *Pressing toward the Mark*. Edited by Charles G. Dennison and Richard C. Gamble. Philadelphia, PA: Committee for the Historian of the Orthodox Presbyterian Church, 1986.

Hoekema, Anthony A. *The Bible and the Future*. Grand Rapids, MI: Eerdmans, 1979.

———. *Created in God's Image*. Grand Rapids, MI: Eerdmans, 1986.

Horton, Michael, *Covenant and Eschatology: The Divine Drama*. Louisville, KY: Westminster John Knox, 2002.

———. *Introducing Covenant Theology*. Grand Rapids, MI: Baker, 2009.

Horton, Michael, Justin Holcomb, Kim Riddlebarger, and Rod Rosenbladt. "The Search for a New Adam." *White Horse Inn* (podcast), June 4, 2017. https://www.whitehorseinn.org/show/the-search-for-a-new-adam-1/.

Jackman, David. "How to Live in Babylon." Sermon, St. Helen's Bishopsgate, London, May 8, 2016. Accessed July 15, 2017. http://www.st-helens.org.uk /resources/media-library/src/talk/54862/title/how-to-live-in-babylon.

Keller, Tim. "Satanic Exposition." Sermon, Redeemer Presbyterian Church, New York, February 1, 2009. Accessed July 11, 2017. https://www.truth forlife.org/resources/sermon/satanic-exposition.

———. "Tale of Two Cities." Sermon, Basics Conference 2015, Parkside Church, Chagrin Falls, OH, May 13, 2015. Accessed May 17, 2015. http:// www.gospelinlife.com/a-tale-of-two-cities-6004.

Kline, Meredith G. *Images of the Spirit*. Eugene, OR: Wipf & Stock, 1999.

———. *Kingdom Prologue: Genesis Foundations for a Covenantal Worldview*. Eugene, OR: Wipf & Stock, 2006.

Lints, Richard. *Identity and Idolatry*. Downers Grove, IL: InterVarsity Press, 2015.

Messner, Aaron. "Remember the Sabbath: The 4th Commandment." Sermon, Covenant College, Lookout Mountain, GA, February 9, 2010. Accessed June 5, 2013.

Ortlund, Dane. "Inaugurated Glorification: Revisiting Romans 8:30." *Journal of the Evangelical Theological Society* 57, no. 1 (2014): 111–33.

Ortlund, Raymond C. *Marriage and the Mystery of the Gospel*. Short Studies in Biblical Theology. Wheaton, IL: Crossway, 2016.

Piper, John. *This Momentary Marriage: A Parable of Permanence*. Wheaton, IL: Crossway, 2009.

———. *Spectacular Sins: And Their Global Purpose in the Glory of Christ*. Wheaton, IL: Crossway, 2013.

Rishmawy, Derek. "9 Reasons the Garden of Eden Was a Temple." *Reformedish* (blog), December 7, 2012. Accessed June 26, 2017. https://derekzrishmawy .com/2012/12/07/9-reasons-the-garden-of-eden-was-a-temple/.

Smith, Colin S. *Unlocking the Bible Story*. Chicago, IL: Moody Press, 2002.

Starke, Robert. "The Tree of Life: Protological to Eschatological." *Kerux: The Journal of Northwest Theological Seminary* 11 (September 1996): 15–31.

Strain, David. "The Seed of the Woman." Sermon, First Presbyterian Church, Jackson, MS, November 27, 2016. Accessed June 19, 2017. http://www .fpcjackson.org/resource-library/sermons/the-seed-of-the-woman.

Taylor, Justin. "Why I Believe in the Covenant of Works." *Between Two Worlds* (blog), The Gospel Coalition, May 11, 2012. Accessed February 24, 2017. https://blogs.thegospelcoalition.org/justintaylor/2012/05/11 /why-i-believe-in-the-covenant-of-works/.

Taylor, William. "Jesus Weeps Over Jerusalem: Luke 19:41–48." Sermon, St. Helen's Bishopsgate, London, December 4, 2005. Accessed July 6, 2017. http://www.st-helens.org.uk/resources/media-library/src/talk /9282/title/jesus-weeps-over-jerusalem.

———. "Marriage 1—God's Purpose in Marriage." Sermon, St. Helen's Bishopsgate, London, January 30, 2001. Accessed June 2, 2017. http:// www.st-helens.org.uk/resources/media-library/src/talk/6313/title /marriage-i-god-s-purpose-in-marriage.

———. "Sodom: Two Responses." Sermon, St. Helen's Bishopsgate, London, February 23, 2014. Accessed July 14, 2017. http://www.st-helens.org.uk /resources/media-library/src/talk/53730/title/sodom-two-responses.

———. "The Temple." Sermon, St. Helen's Bishopsgate, London, September 2003. Accessed June 30, 2017. http://www.st-helens.org.uk /resources/media-library/src/talk/7970/title/5-the-temple.

Tipton, Lane. "The Archetypal Image in Colossians 1:15: Theological Implications." Lecture, 2016 Reformed Forum Theology Conference, Hope Orthodox Presbyterian Church, Grayslake, IL, October 8, 2016. Accessed May 20, 2017. http://reformedforum.org/rf16_05_tipton/.

———. "The Covenant of Works: Adam's Destiny." Lecture, ST131: Survey of Reformed Theology, Westminster Theological Seminary, Philadelphia, PA, March 25, 2015.

———. "The Image of God: Biblical-Theological Foundations." Lecture, 2016 Reformed Forum Theology Conference, Hope Orthodox Presbyterian Church, Grayslake, IL, October 15, 2016. Accessed May 18, 2017. http://reformedforum.org/category/series/events /2016-theology-conference/.

Tipton, Lane, and Camden Bucey. "Vos Group #5: The Content of Pre-Redemptive Special Revelation, Part 1." *Reformed Forum* (audioblog), May 2, 2014. Accessed March 19, 2017. http://reformedforum.org/ctc331/.

Vos, Geerhardus. *Biblical Theology: Old and New Testaments*. Eugene, OR: Wipf & Stock, 2003.

———. *The Eschatology of the Old Testament*. Phillipsburg, NJ: P&R, 2001.

Wilder, William N. "Illumination and Investiture: The Royal Significance of the Tree of Wisdom in Genesis 3." *Westminster Theological Journal* 68 (2006): 51–69.

Williams, Paul. "You Will Trample the Serpent." Sermon, All Souls Langham Place, London, April 9, 2005. Accessed June 25, 2017. http://all souls.org/Media/AllMedia.aspx.

Willson, Mary. "The Sabbath: A Biblical Theological Approach." Lecture, The Gospel Coalition Women's Conference, Orlando, FL, June 23, 2012. Accessed May 22, 2017. http://resources.thegospelcoalition.org /library/the-sabbath.

Wood, Will, Camden Bucey, and Jared Oliphant. "Ephesians 6:10–17 and a Biblical Theology of Clothing." *Reformed Forum* (audioblog), April 1, 2016. Accessed April 8, 2016. http://reformedforum.org/ctc431/.

Wright, Christopher. "He Casts Down Babylon." Sermon, All Souls Langham Place, London, July 8, 2012. Accessed July 11, 2017. http://www.all souls.org/Media/Player.aspx?media_id=91600&file_id=100776.

General Index

Aaron, 52
Abraham: call of, 19; covenant with, 128; promise to, 97–98
Adam: covenant obligations of, 180n5; failure of, 97; sense of self, 48–49; work of, 96. *See also* Adam and Eve
Adam and Eve: allegiance of, 57; clothed by God, 65; death of, 175n11; discontentment of, 17–19; disobedience of, 12; exile of, 19, 161; experience of, 13; failure of, 49, 65; glory of, 49; God's intention for, 63, 65; God's plan for, 70; God's purpose for, 97; as image bearers, 55; as marred image of God, 49–50; marriage of, 79–82, 90; nakedness of, 62, 64, 177n3; offspring of, 114–16; spiritual death of, 36; and tree of life, 175n7; work of, 18
ark of the covenant, 130, 133, 183n2

Babel, as city of man, 146–47
Babylon: as city of man, 150–52, 155; destiny of, 155; destruction of, 155–56; as God's tool, 150; idolatries of, 155; spiritual city in, 150–51
baptism, sign of, 105
Bible, the: genealogies in, 114; as love story, 77; story of, 12, 27, 145

bronze serpent, 115, 182n4
Brown, Pearl, 30, 41–42, 43

Cain: birth of, 97; and city of man, 146; descendant of Satan, 114, 182n7.3; jealousy of, 81–82; mark on, 145; rage of, 114
Cain and Abel, 114, 145–46. *See also* Cain
childbirth, pain of, 81
church, the, as the new temple, 138
circumcision, sign of, 105
city of God, 145; future of, 151; promises of, 152; spiritual, 146
city of man, 145; in Eden, 145; greed of, 145; marks of, 145
clothing: anticipation of, 71–74; function of, 177n3; of the high priest, 65–66; as holiness, beauty, and glory, 69, 71, 73; of immortality, 63, 72; of Jesus, 67; promise of, 66–68; of righteousness, 64; thinking about, 71
contentment: in the new garden, 27–28; in the wilderness, 22–27
corruption, of priests, 66
covenant: with Abraham, 128; everlasting, 128; heart of, 128; of redemption, 137; signs of, 104; of works, 174n1.4, 174n2.2; 174n2.3, 180n4; first, 177n5
cross, the: fruit of, 40; as tree, 39

Scripture Index